'The style is lively and lucid . . . it brings impressively to life the personalities of each of the Habsburgs' – *Scotsman*

'An admirable study, lively and replete with information, yet reflective' – *Financial Times*

'Interesting personal details as well as a vivid account of the general history of the monarchy from 1273 to 1918' – *Yorkshire Post*

Other biographies published by Corgi

Edward Crankshaw

The Habsburgs

CORGI BOOKS
A DIVISION OF TRANSWORLD PUBLISHERS LTD
A NATIONAL GENERAL COMPANY

THE HABSBURGS

A CORGI BOOK o 552 09068 X

Originally published in Great Britain
by George Weidenfeld and Nicolson Ltd.

PRINTING HISTORY
Weidenfeld and Nicolson edition published 1971
Corgi edition published 1972

Corgi Books are published by Transworld
Publishers Ltd.,
Cavendish House, 57–59 Uxbridge Road,
Ealing, London W.5.
Made and printed in Great Britain by
Cox & Wyman Ltd., London, Reading and Fakenham

**NOTE: The Australian price appearing on the
back cover is the recommended retail price.**

CONTENTS

LIST OF ILLUSTRATIONS AND ACKNOWLEDGMENTS

Emperor Joseph II with his brother Archduke Ferdinand, painted by
   Batoni in 1769
   (Österreichische Nationalbibliothek (Bildarchiv), Vienna)

Emperor Francis I riding with his queen, the Bavarian princess, Caroline
   Augusta
   (Österreichische Nationalbibliothek (Bildarchiv), Vienna)

The allied troops enter Paris in 1814, Emperors Alexander and Frederick
   William at their head
   (Heeresgeschichtliches Museum, Vienna)

A Viennese student reads aloud, to the cheers of the crowd, the constitution which student revolutionaries drew up as part of their
   demands for reform, March 13th 1848
   (Historisches Museum der Stadt Wien)

March 17th, 1848, the national flag is hauled up by Italian rebels in St.
   Mark's Square, Venice
   (Österreichische Nationalbibliothek (Bildarchiv), Vienna)

The National Guard fires on the Viennese rebels
   (Österreichische Nationalbibliothek (Bildarchiv), Vienna)

The Cartoonists image of the National Guard during the uprising in
   Vienna
   (Historisches Museum der Stadt Wien)

A cartoon in *Punch* called 'Dropping the Pilot' mirrored public reaction
   to the decision of the young Kaiser William II to dismiss Bismark
   (Punch, *London*)

The state car in which Francis Ferdinand and his wife drove through the
   streets of Sarajevo. A few minutes later they were assassinated
   (Popperfoto, London)

The lying in state of the Habsburg heir, and his wife Sophie Chotek
   (Press Association, London)

The foundation of a dynasty: Rudolph I; Frederick III

THERE was a brooding quality about many of the Habsburgs which distinguished them from the general run of monarchs and enhanced the image of their power, an image compounded largely of Catholic bigotry and Imperial reaction. It was a quality fixed for ever in Titian's portrait of the Emperor Charles V. Charles for a time was the mightiest ruler since the Romans. He was master of all Central Europe, of Burgundy and the Netherlands, of most of Italy, of Spain, of all the Spanish possessions in the New World. But he was the least showy of monarchs. He dressed simply, and after the death of his wife always in black. With all his unrivalled grandeur, he presented himself invariably as a human being, and he was content to be immortalized as such by his beloved Titian, to whom he sat five times. It is an individual, brooding, complex, strong yet vulnerable, whose private mystery is described in these portraits, but not elucidated. And somehow the weight of the immense power embodied in this individual is made to seem more frightening and terrible – perhaps more preposterous – by the absence of panache and outward show.

This rejection of outward show, except when assumed for specific ritual occasions, ran through the family for century on century. So we have Philip II of Spain presiding over the Inquisition and bringing his might against England, Ferdinand II of Austria, dourly conducting the Counter-Reformation and the Thirty Years' War, men controlling the destinies of millions, men served by the most ostentatious nobility in Christendom, conducting their business as sombrely dressed, conscientious and hardworking bureaucrats, dwelling in monastic simplicity at the heart of splendour. So we have Leopold I of Austria embattled against

Louis XIV on the one hand and Ottoman power on the other, Carlyle's 'little black *Herr* in red stockings', devoting his leisure hours to musical composition and performance. So we have the last great Habsburg, Francis Joseph, sleeping on his narrow iron bed amid the glories of Schönbrunn, for decade after decade toiling quietly at his desk to support the glittering panoply of Imperial Vienna and to hold together a vast Empire and sustain an ancient dynasty, both of which were to collapse just two years after his death. Yet it was this same Francis Joseph who at the beginning of his reign gloried in the white tunics of his Imperial and Royal Army which, for western liberals, became the very symbol of repression and autocratic rule.

Who were these Habsburgs? Where did they come from? What force sustained them to make them the oldest dynasty in Europe? One has only to reflect a moment to realize that the old liberal image of a greedy and arrogant autocracy tyrannizing over a prison-house of nations will not do. In the early years of this century it was easy to believe that when Habsburg power was broken the many peoples of that polyglot Empire, emerging into freedom, would march triumphantly and steadily towards the light. But this did not happen. The Habsburgs were all too soon followed by the dictators. First the national dictatorships in lands once wholly or partly ruled by Habsburg – in Hungary, in Yugoslavia, in Poland, in the rump of Austria itself: only in Czechoslovakia was a firm democracy established, to be destroyed first by Hitler, then by Stalin. The Czechs indeed had much to complain of at the hands of Austria, but at least they breathed and grew. It was a Czech revolutionary nationalist, the historian Palacky, who, while fighting Habsburg absolutism, could yet stand back and understand that the Habsburg Empire made sense. Paraphrasing Voltaire's remark on God, he exclaimed that if Austria had not existed it would have been necessary to invent her. Austria was Habsburg.

It is worth going back in time to examine the truth of this. The story of Austria is, above all, the story of an extraordinary family. The Habsburg tenure of Spain was an interlude – under Charles V and Philip II a dazzling and grandiose interlude by all means. It could not last. Spain, anyway, was beginning to move towards a dead-end even under Philip III. The real story of the Habsburgs is the story of the House of Austria; and this story is central to the story of modern Europe – that is to say, to the development of our western culture and society, which gave birth also to the New World.

The Habsburg connection with Austria was established in 1276, but it took another two hundred years for Austria to emerge as a major force in the development of Europe, and on more than one occasion during that time it looked as though the line would sink into the oblivion from which it had emerged with the first Imperial Habsburg, Rudolph I, crowned King of the Germans at Aix-la-Chapelle in 1273.*

It is needless to dwell in detail on the lives and wildly fluctuating fortunes of the medieval Habsburgs. They were warring princes, distinguished from other warring princes of the thirteenth and fourteenth centuries occasionally by their ability, almost invariably by their extreme tenacity of purpose. Their characters need not engage us more than a little, partly because their attitudes and circumstances were so remote from our own, partly because we do not and cannot know them well enough, partly because their impact on the development of Europe was small. There were also too many of them: until the middle of the fifteenth century their lands, themselves small, and largely mountainous at that, were divided again and again among quarrelling brothers. What matters is that they survived, perpetuated their line, and managed to hold on until, in 1493, Maximilian I quite suddenly emerged as the master and symbol of an important European power.

What also matters is to have some sort of a picture of the European structure which hemmed them in. For when, in due course, they broke out, it was to impose their rule on a number of peoples with ancient national histories behind them. To a greater or lesser

* The revival of the Roman Empire, created by Charlemagne as part of his dream of uniting all Christendom under one temporal head, and to become known as the Holy Roman Empire, had long ceased to mean much in terms of power. But the Emperor was still vested with a quasi-mystical authority, even though he was now little more than the elected figurehead, or King, of the German peoples.

degree these peoples preserved legendary memories of their pre-Habsburg pasts. When, after the Napoleonic Wars, the great age of nationalism dawned, it was to their medieval kings that Czechs, Serbs, Croats, Hungarians and Poles looked back for inspiration in their struggle with the Imperial government in Vienna.

The Habsburgs were Germans. They can be traced back with certainty to the tenth century, in the person of Guntram the Rich, Count of Alsace. They took their name in the eleventh century from the *Habichtsburg*, or Falcon's Castle, which stood dourly at the confluence of the Aar and the Rhine in present-day Switzerland. Among their contemporary princes established in the same general region were the Wittelsbachs, an even more ancient family, who were to become kings of Bavaria, and the Hohenzollerns, who were to transfer themselves to Brandenburg in North Germany, become kings of Prussia and, in the end, Emperors of the unified German Reich. The early Habsburgs were faithful servants of the Imperial crown, and one of them won particular favour for his support of the last great Hohenstaufen Emperor, Frederick II, in his losing struggle with the Pope.

When Frederick died in 1250, the great Sicilian who had earned the title *Stupor mundi* for the brilliance and culture of his court, now broken and excommunicated like so many of his predecessors, it was the end of the Holy Roman Empire as a coherent and active power. For a long time Charlemagne's dream of a unified Christendom had been fading. In practice, until Frederick, successive Emperors had been little more than kings of the Germans, enjoying great prestige and wielding considerable authority over the multitudinous principalities, secular and episcopal, into which the area now most of Germany, Czechoslovakia, Alsace, Austria and part of Switzerland was divided. With Frederick out of the way, the Pope decided to keep Germany enfeebled, divided and torn with strife. The Imperial title was turned into a mockery. One of the shadow Emperors was Richard of Cornwall, son of the English King John. But the German Electors had so little use for this absentee liege lord that they held a counter-election, choosing Alphonso of Castile. Then, two years after Richard's death in 1272, Pope Gregory X, reversing his predecessor's policies, decided to put an end to chaos in Germany and restore some dignity to the

Imperial crown. He refused to recognize the validity of Alphonso's claim and told the Electors that if they did not pull themselves together and choose a new German king in accordance with the proper forms, he himself would do it for them. The Electors chose Count Rudolph of Habsburg, and the Pope approved the choice. He was chosen not because he was strong but because, although a warrior prince of outstanding talents with a reputation for benevolence and enlightenment, he was weak. That is to say, he lacked a sufficiently powerful base to dominate his fellow princes. These would support him when it was convenient to them, but they stood in no danger of finding themselves subjected to his will.

The new Emperor was fifty-five and he had a lifetime of fighting behind him. He had fought not only to secure and extend his own small dominions but also, in engagement after engagement, to put down the bandit lords who, proliferating in those anarchic times, pillaged the countryside and oppressed the burghers and the peasantry as they fought among themselves. Rudolph was indeed possessed of a strong sense of the need for order and equity. He was good at raising temporary allies for the prosecution of his personal campaigns. He knew how to mature large plans and to carry them out with minimal resources, moving decisively and swiftly and achieving his objectives with the aid of unconventional stratagems and devices which showed a touch of genius. One of his achievements was a surprise crossing of the Danube on a bridge of boats; he was believed to have been the first man to hit on this devastatingly simple expedient since Alexander the Great. On another occasion, laying siege to a castle, he observed that at regular intervals a party of foragers on grey horses made a sortie through the castle gates into the surrounding countryside. This suggested a plan. He mounted the same number of his own men on grey horses and held them ready. One afternoon, when the foraging party had emerged and trotted off into the landscape, he set off his own party at a resounding gallop towards the castle gates, hotly pursuing them with a large detachment. The garrison guard, catching the alarm, flung open the gates to admit the grey horsemen, and slammed them shut in the faces of the 'pursuers'. The infiltrators made short work of the unfortunate guard and opened the gate to Rudolph's whole army. So this Habsburg was cunning as well as ingenious and brave.

When the news of his election was brought to him, he was laying siege to Basel where a contumelious bishop had engineered an uprising against him. Ironically, the news was brought by a young Hohenzollern, who was thus the first to bow the knee to the first Habsburg Emperor, and the ancestor of a later Hohenzollern who, with Bismarck at his elbow and Moltke commanding his army, was, almost six centuries later, to drive Austria out of Germany.

The Bishop of Basel, when he heard what had happened, is said to have exclaimed: 'Sit fast, Lord God, or Rudolph will also have Thy throne!'

As for Rudolph himself, after his coronation at Aix-la-Chapelle, which had very much the aspect of a religious sacrament, he said: 'I am no longer the man you knew before.' He meant, and he no doubt believed it, that as the Lord's anointed he was thenceforth dedicated to the service of Christendom. But his words were also prophetic in the secular sphere.

The citizens of Basel, willing if not eager to fight for their bishop against a Count of Habsburg, had no desire to stand out against an elected Emperor. And so it was with others who had fought Rudolph in the past. With his own lands and the neighbouring territories subdued by the mystique of the Imperial crown, he turned to larger things.

The man who had confidently expected to be elected Emperor was a very different sort of prince. He was the King of Bohemia, Ottocar Przemysl II. Bohemia was the last Slav kingdom to remain an effective part of the Empire, and Ottocar was far more powerful than any of the German princes, who, naturally, did not want him on their backs. This Ottocar had built up a very considerable empire in Central and Eastern Europe. He ranged from Croatia on the Adriatic in the south to the Baltic in the north. Quite recently Ottocar had also seized Austria and Styria, Carinthia, Carniola and the Windisch Mark, provinces which made up Charlemagne's Ostmark, the borderland outpost against the Magyars and other predatory peoples coming out of the East. He was a very formidable man indeed and he regarded Rudolph of Habsburg, with his tiny estates, with perfect contempt, refusing to recognize him as Emperor, refusing to pay his dues. Out of this conflict grew Habsburg Austria. It was also the effective beginning of the long, sad history of strife between the German Austrians and the western Slavs.

Very quickly Rudolph collected together enough supporters to march an army down the Danube to Vienna. Here he wasted no time in sapping and mining and sitting down to starve the Viennese. As always, he hit on the most direct and economical expedient. If the Viennese refused to open their gates and admit their Emperor, he would be reluctantly compelled to destroy the vineyards which, then as now, covered the gentle slopes leading up to the Vienna Woods. The Viennese, realists, opened their gates. Ottocar agreed to surrender his Austrian possessions, including the fine church of St. Stephen, later to be a cathedral, which he had been rebuilding, and retire to Prague.

Rudolph was not a stranger to him. In earlier days the young Habsburg had fought under him in the famous campaign, a crusade it was called, which the Bohemian king had mounted against the barbarians of Prussia. Meeting him again, he was no doubt impressed by the character and vitality of this large, beaky man, who was, when all was said, his appointed liege lord.

Ottocar had no right to Austria: it was in the gift of the Emperor, and he had simply moved in when the Babenberg line had died out and there was no effective Emperor in being. But he had no intention of giving up the struggle. He would agree now to an accommodation; he would even give his blessing to the betrothal of two of his children to two of Rudolph's. He needed only time to organize an army which would quickly put an end to this Habsburg pretender. He, Ottocar, was a king, with all the resources of his very large realm to draw upon. Rudolph might be Emperor, but he depended absolutely on the troops he could raise by cajolery, moral blackmail, or the promise of favours to come from the German principalities: he would be hard put to it to oppose Ottocar with sufficient force to avoid disaster, let alone win victory. And, indeed, the new Emperor was hard put to it. It was

15

Ottocar who made the running and chose the time. In 1278 he appeared with a formidable army in the flat land across the great river from Vienna. Rudolph was heavily outnumbered, but it was against his character to wait for Ottocar to attack. Instead, he managed to get his forces across the Danube and, benefiting by surprise, shattered the Bohemians and killed Ottocar himself at the battle of the Marchfeld. The Emperor had asserted himself. More relevantly to the future, the Habsburgs had Austria. Before very long Rudolph, who had seized the Austrian lands in his capacity as Emperor, transferred them to his family. Carinthia went to Count Meinhardt of Tyrol as a reward for his support against Ottocar; the rest of the lands were divided between Rudolph's two sons. Germans, not Slavs, henceforth were to hold the key to Central Europe.

Vienna was very much a key. It was above all a frontier fortress. And the Marchfeld across the river was traditionally a battlefield. It was to remain so.

Vienna lies sheltered by the last north-eastern foothills of the Alps, in the angle made by steep and thickly wooded hills and the Danube. Rising in the Black Forest, far to the West, the great river has flowed at the foot of the alpine wall, fed by its snows. Now it winds out across the vast open plain, merging, with virtually no interruption, into the Hungarian *puszta*. The original castle of the Babenbergs, margraves then dukes, established by the Emperor Otto II to hold Charlemagne's border province, the Ostmark, against invasion from the East, stood below the Leopoldsberg, rising high above the river, commanding an infinite view of the great plain which from time immemorial had been the highway for predatory eastern peoples, as for the Turks. The Romans had had an important fortress on this site, and Marcus Aurelius had died in Vienna, the Roman Vindobona. They had fought the Marcomanni on the Marchfeld itself. Under the Swabian Emperors the Babenbergs had transformed the fortress into a city of some mark and cultural fame. Walter von der Vogelweide had brought to their court his songs of chivalry. The Danube plain was not only an invitation for invaders; it was also a route for crusaders. Richard Lionheart, returning from the crusades, had been taken prisoner and held to ransom by the Babenbergs in the castle at

Dürnstein across the river, running here between steep cliffs, from their original capital at Pöchlarn. But in the tenth century it, and all Austria and much of Bavaria, had been overrun by the Magyars at the limit of their extraordinary westward drive from the banks of the river Ob in deep Siberia until, in 955, they were shattered by Otto the Great at the Battle of the Lechfeld, near Augsburg in Bavaria, one of the decisive battles of European history. They were pushed back hundreds of miles to the east on the Danube plain, and it was the task of the Babenbergs to hold them there. Now the Habsburgs took over that task, and the Magyars were still strong.

All Eastern Europe, indeed, was in a very interesting condition and one of great fluidity. With Ottocar dead, the great Slav kingdom of Bohemia ceased to be the preponderant power. Far away beyond the Carpathians Kiev Russia with its Christian culture, its connections with Byzantium and its close contacts with the West, had lately been submerged and utterly cut off by the invading Tatars, the 'Golden Horde' under Batu, the grandson of Genghiz Khan. The Russians, eastern Slavs, were to remain thus isolated for two hundred and fifty years, until the final emergence of Muscovy in 1480.

But there were other ancient Slav kingdoms. Poland, which had once been part of the Empire, was diminished by perpetual subdivision, until it became the stamping ground first of the Tatars, then of the Teutonic knights. Bulgaria had been reduced by the Serbs. But Serbia was very much a rising power, profiting by the decline of Bohemia, and was soon to dominate the Balkans, reaching its apogee in the early fourteenth century under the hero King Stepan Dushan, who was planning the conquest of Constantinople when he died. The Magyar kingdom of Hungary, although pushed back from the West, still enjoyed the advanced and unified constitution established in the eleventh century by King Stephen, who was later canonized. The Magyars were to prove an enduring menace to the Habsburgs – to the point of capturing Vienna itself and driving out the Habsburg Emperor, Frederick III, nearly two hundred years after Rudolph. In a word, when the Habsburgs established themselves in Vienna there was no knowing what would happen. The pattern was far from set, and it could by no means be taken for granted that a German princely family could permanently overcome either Magyars or Slavs.

As for the rest of Europe, Germany under its new Emperor was still a welter of quarrelling principalities. Rudolph was able to secure the Imperial crown for his son Albert, but when Albert died in 1308 there was to be no Habsburg Emperor for over a hundred years: the title alternated between Bavaria and Luxembourg.

In the far North, Sweden's struggle for supremacy in Scandinavia did not affect the rest of Europe, though, much later, the great Swedish king Gustavus Adolphus was to checkmate a later Habsburg's fanatical drive to win all Germany back from Rome. In the far South, Italy was moving into the age of the despots. The Low Countries were still fragmented. Switzerland did not exist, its various parts forming part of the Empire: it was only after Rudolph's death that the first three forest cantons achieved the union which was to form the nucleus of an independent Switzerland. But farther to the west the beginnings of modern Europe were taking shape. France and England were on the way to becoming unified nation states, identified with their own kings. Edward I in England had recently subdued the Welsh. The terrible struggle between the French king in Paris and the Counts of Toulouse, disguised as a war of religion, had ended with the fall of Mont Ségur in 1245 and the extirpation of the Albigensian heresy, while the massacres of Montpellier and Béziers had sealed in blood the effective unification of northern and southern France. The Hundred Years' War was yet to come, was indeed to be fought out during the period when the Habsburgs were consolidating their hold on Austria and preparing for the great leap forward. Southern Spain with Granada was still in the hands of the Moors, who had been established there for five hundred years; but, in the north, Castile had lately absorbed Navarre and León, leaving only Aragon to its starveling independence for another two hundred years. The Turks had not yet crossed the Straits into Europe, and the idea of the mighty Ottoman Empire, which was to seize Constantinople, absorb the Balkans, shatter the power of Serbia, overrun Hungary and lap the walls of Vienna itself was yet unborn.

This was the Europe in which Habsburg power had its beginnings and might well have met its end. For a hundred years after the death of Rudolph the Habsburgs hung on to Austria, frequently quarrelling, above all among themselves, and building up their individual centres of power at Graz in Styria and Innsbruck in the Tyrol. During this period they were, in the main, oblivious of the larger European movements, and one Habsburg after another expended his energy in vain, battering against the newly self-conscious Swiss, a long-drawn-out struggle that was to give rise, among other things, to the legend of William Tell. The most interesting of the fourteenth-century Habsburgs was Rudolph IV, known as Rudolph the Founder. As Duke of Austria he acquired the Tyrol and, in 1365, founded the University of Vienna, pre-dating by eighteen years the University of Prague. Vienna, thus, while still very much a frontier town, was establishing itself also as the cultural capital of the future realm. It was this Rudolph, too, who began the enlargement of St. Stephen's Cathedral, widening the great nave to prepare for its final form. Even so, the Habsburg lands were again divided on Rudolph's death. Not for another hundred years was the Emperor Maximilian I to establish undisputed mastery of all the Habsburg possessions in their entirety – and to add mightily to them.

During all this time medieval Europe was being hammered out into more or less the final form which was to endure until the twentieth century. It was an age of perpetual movement. Emperors, kings, princes, prince bishops, knights and men-at-arms made incessant and incredible journeys, brilliantly apparelled on their heavy horses, joining in constantly changing alliances, combining the business of their imperial, royal or princely masters with their pursuit of private gain, pausing to draw up a battle-line and putting on their heavy armour to confront the enemy of the moment, meeting each other in elaborate tournaments when there was no battle to be fought, journeying over roads, over snowy mountain passes from one end of Europe to the other to make an advantageous marriage, unfolding their silken tents, streaming their pennants and banners, setting out their gold and silver plate all carried in their baggage trains like so many travelling circuses.

While the princes, as a rule, kept their dignity, their loutish followers kept up a tumult of brawling and noisy quarrelling, duelling and murder.

The Holy Roman Emperor, at least as King of the Germans, was still very much a personage, and the seven Electors who chose him enjoyed real power. When the second Habsburg Emperor died in 1308 the election went to a Count of Luxembourg, a Frenchman in speech and sympathy, Henry VII. And it was this Henry to whom Dante, in exile, and the Ghibelline party in Italy, looked for a reassertion of the Empire over the papal Guelfs – proof enough that the Imperial idea was still very much alive in the best minds of the day. But Henry was not up to a task which in fact had become impossible. The crown went in 1313 to Louis of Bavaria.

Meanwhile the early medieval dynasties of Eastern Europe were dying out. The Przemysl line of Bohemia, Ottocar's line, had come to an end, and it was Henry's son, John, Count of Luxembourg, who was elected King of Bohemia in 1310. John did not like Bohemia. He left Prague to look after itself and embarked on a career of endless journeying and campaigning until, blind in early middle-age, but still fighting, he was killed in 1346 at the Battle of Crécy when his kinsman Philip VI of France was overwhelmingly defeated by the English under Edward III and the Black Prince, in one of the most spectacular episodes of the great struggle between France and England known as the Hundred Years' War.

The point to be made is the extreme fluidity of Europe at this time and the interchangeability of its ruling families. These were still cosmopolitan. Just as the Counts of Luxembourg were now ruling in Prague, so, with the extinction of the Arpad dynasty of the Magyars, the Dukes of Anjou were ruling in Hungary, and Louis the Great of Hungary was soon to bestow the kingdom of Poland on one of his daughters. The Europe of the middle twentieth century is parochial in the extreme compared with this Europe of an earlier age, which recognized few national frontiers, but only the personal fiefs of embattled princes whose families were closely interwoven. But for the Tatar conquest, the vast hinterland of Russia would have also formed part of this complex, distance notwithstanding. It is worth remembering that in the eleventh century an English princess was betrothed to a Russian prince of Kiev.

The Luxembourg interest in Bohemia is not irrelevant to the Habsburg story. It led directly to Habsburg rule in Prague. Blind King John, who died at Crécy, had a son, Charles, who was luckier than his father. Born in Prague, but still very much a Frenchman, and married to a daughter of the French king, Philip VI, Charles nevertheless set out to make the best of his inheritance and worked hard to build up Bohemian culture and trade. After him was named the famous Charles University which, as a repository of Czech national tradition, was to become a symbol for heroic Czech resistance to Russia nearly six hundred years later. He also succeeded Louis of Bavaria, in 1347, as Emperor Charles IV. And it was he who published the celebrated Golden Bull of 1356 which fixed, for ever it was thought, the composition, privileges and duties of the Electoral College which held the future of the Empire in its hands.*

In 1378 Charles was succeeded both as Emperor and King of Bohemia by his son Wenceslaus IV, who was so ineffective and unpopular that his halfbrother Sigismund seized power, holding Wenceslaus prisoner for a time, and in due course formally succeeding him in 1411. This Sigismund, who married the Hungarian queen (or king as she had to be called according to the old Magyar custom) Mary, daughter of Louis the Great, was a formidable man, a born fighter who found himself from the beginning closely involved with affairs of religion. At the turn of the century the scandal of the papacy (there were no fewer than three popes at odds with one another) had become intolerable, and Sigismund made it his first business to put an end to it. At the same time he had thrust upon him the difficult affair of John Hus, the reforming Bohemian cleric who, inspired by Wycliffe's teachings, had become a Czech national hero. It was Sigismund who gave Hus

* These were the Elector Palatine, the Duke of Saxony, the Margrave of Brandenburg, the King of Bohemia, the Archbishops of Mainz, Cologne and Trier. The clerics were Archchancellors for the kingdoms of Germany, Italy and Burgundy. The Elector Palatine was the Emperor's steward, the Duke of Saxony his Marshal, the Margrave of Brandenburg his Chamberlain, the King of Bohemia his cup-bearer. The Dukes of Austria were not Electors. It was only later that the Habsburgs had a vote as Kings of Bohemia.

his safe conduct to attend the Council of Constance to defend himself against the charge of heresy. And it was Sigismund who was blamed for treachery when Hus was seized and tried and burnt at Constance in 1415, a martyrdom which led to a national uprising in Bohemia and the savage Hussite war which dragged on for seventeen years, laying waste a prospering land and sowing the seeds of enduring hatred. Sigismund, ruler of Hungary by marriage, relied very much on Hungarian support in crushing his Bohemian nationalist and pre-Protestant rebels, and the consequent ill-feeling between Czech and Magyar (later augmented by other actions) has endured to this day. Sigismund also received active and vigorous support from the Habsburg Duke of Austria, Albert V. And it was as a direct consequence of this that Albert was nominated King of the Germans and crowned as the Emperor Albert II when Sigismund died in 1437. Thereafter, save for a short interval from 1742–5, the Imperial crown was to be the perquisite of the Habsburgs until the formal dissolution of the Holy Roman Empire under pressure from Napoleon in 1806. Imperial Austria was thus founded upon the humiliation of the Czechs and had its origin in support of Catholic orthodoxy against a great reforming movement which was a precursor of the Reformation proper.

Even so, when Albert was elected in 1438 nothing could have looked less secure than the imperial future of the Habsburgs. A year later he was dead of dysentery, aggravated by a surfeit of melons consumed in a river-campaign against the Turks. He had a posthumous son who died at eighteen, and meanwhile the duchy had gone to his nephew Frederick, who was elected Emperor in 1440, as Frederick III, to embark on a fifty-three-year reign of ignominy and disaster. He was so feeble, indecisive and lethargic that he was unable even to put a stop to the claims of his younger brother to the Duchy of Austria, who defied his authority until his death in 1463. Frederick himself had strong claims to the thrones of Bohemia and Hungary, but he was quite incapable of enforcing them. Worse still, he lost Austria, Styria and Carinthia to a new and aggressive Magyar king, Matthew Corvinus, son of Janos Corvinus Hunyadi, a Hungarian warrior who had risen high under the

Emperor Sigismund in the Hussite Wars, placed Ladislaus III of Poland on the Hungarian throne, and been elected Governor of Hungary when Ladislaus was killed by the Turks in the crushing defeat at Varna in 1444. Matthew Corvinus ranged far and wide, drove back the Turks in the East, overran Bohemia in the North and, in the end, threatened the Habsburg inheritance with extinction. He built up Buda and revived the Magyar university, but at the close of his life he was living in Vienna, whence Frederick had fled.

How Frederick survived in the face of the Hungarian peril, and many others too, it is impossible to imagine. Perhaps the simple answer is that he was above all, perhaps solely, a survivor. All his actions suggest that his metabolism was extremely low, and this enabled him to live through defeats and humiliations that would have killed a livelier man, as fish may live when their pond is frozen into a solid block of ice.

He was intelligent. That brilliant, passionate, humane and questing careerist, Pope Pius II, found it worthwhile, in his early thirties, to enter into his close service as the young Aeneas Sylvius Piccolomini. Frederick thus achieved immortality in Pintoricchio's great frescoes of the life of Pius II in the Piccolomini Library of the cathedral at Siena. And Aeneas Sylvius spoke up loudly for his hopeless master. In a former address to the Germans he summed up the situation once and for all:

> Although you acknowledge the Emperor for your king and master, he possesses but a precarious sovereignty; he has no power; you obey him only when you choose; and you are seldom inclined to obey. You are all desirous to be free; neither the princes nor the states render him what is due; he has no revenues, no treasure. Hence you are involved in endless wars and contests; hence also rapine, murder, conflagrations, and a thousand evils which arise from divided authority.

The future Pope was not exaggerating. Frederick had so little power and money that on his journey to Rome for his coronation (he was the last Emperor to be crowned in Rome), travelling through country of which he was supreme temporal head, he could not muster a large enough retinue to defend his person against any

23

inconsiderable body of lawless men who cared to fall upon him. But even though he lacked power and money and men, respect for the Imperial crown was strong enough to see him through unscathed.

The odd thing about this strange but likeable man was a kind of inspired and stubborn optimism, tinged with mysticism, which, depending on miracles, was in the end justified by the miracle taking place. For this he deserves some credit. He was the first Habsburg to be seized with the sense of his family's high and inescapable destiny. Losing Bohemia, losing Hungary, losing Austria itself, driven from his capital, Vienna, utterly penniless in the end, he nevertheless was sustained by a vision of the future. He proved to his own satisfaction that he was a direct descendant of King Priam of Troy. Everything he owned (it was not much) he had stamped or engraved with the mysterious initials, AEIOU. After his death in 1493 the legend took root that these puzzling vowels meant: *Austriae est Imperare Orbi Universo, or 'Alles Edreich ist Oesterreich untherthan'.* For a man in his situation this was the oddest thought imaginable. But by the time of his death it was making at least a flicker of sense. For Frederick had achieved two things besides surviving. In 1459 he fathered a son, Maximilian, who was to outshine in his person all his ancestors, and, with really remarkable foresight and persistence, he laid the foundations for the marriage of that son to Marie of Burgundy, thus bringing the Habsburgs into the mainstream of European history as it emerged from the Middle Ages. Having survived political extinction by a miracle, they were never to look back.

2

The Burgundian inheritance:
Maximilian I

MAXIMILIAN I has been called the last of the knights. This is fair enough as far as it goes. It was as a champion of chivalry that he liked to present himself and wanted to be remembered: he was that very rare creature, a reigning monarch who wrote his own personal memoirs. He also left behind a large, fascinating and attractive body of personal correspondence. There was to be nothing like this in Austria until his remote descendant, the Empress Maria Theresa, his equal in vitality and vivacity, talkativeness too, composed her own memorials, or testaments, and bombarded her family and friends with an unceasing flow of advice, news, endearments, encouragement, exhortation, anecdote and criticism in the second half of the eighteenth century. He was gay, humorous and reckless, an exhibitionist who could laugh at himself.

I have danced a good deal, and tilted lances and enjoyed carnival, [he wrote to an intimate]. I have paid court to the ladies and earned great thanks; for the most part I have laughed heartily. But in tilting I've fallen so often that I could scarcely take courage again; no lady will love me from the heart alone ... Now it is Lent, and I know not what to confess, for all I have done in this carnival time confesses itself.

Maria Theresa in her time was to write in much the same vein; but in her time it was riding and dancing and cards. She would have enjoyed Maximilian, separated from her by three centuries. He and she were the only ruling Habsburgs who threw themselves into life and tried to swallow it whole. But there was much more in both of them than that.

The Maximilian we know broods with hooded eyes in Dürer's great portrait painted two months before the Emperor's death, in 1519, at the age of sixty. He has the first Rudolph's great beak of a nose; he also has that deformity of the lower jaw and lip which had been introduced into the family by the apparently indestructible genes of the Polish Princess Cymburga of Masovia, who was said to be a great beauty notwithstanding, and with whom Maximilian's grandfather, Ernest, had fallen passionately in love. Ernest was so tough that he was known as the 'Iron Duke'; Cymburga was so strong that she could hammer a nail into a board with her bare hands. Perhaps this remarkable parentage was in itself enough to explain the introverted and retiring nature of poor Frederick. Maximilian threw back to her: he could bend a horseshoe with his hands.

It was when Maximilian was only fourteen that his father embarked in earnest on his great design. Burgundy was still very much a power in Europe. It consisted now of what was left of an older Duchy, roughly present-day Burgundy, with Dijon as its capital and the Franche Comté, centred on Dôle, together with the greater part of the rich lands of Flanders and Brabant, Luxembourg, and the outlying provinces of Picardy and Artois. Charles the Rash of Burgundy, gifted, reckless, cultured, intensely ambitious, had to resign himself to the fact that he would never be master of France, which his father Philip the Good, whose cold and calculating features were so wonderfully recorded by the Flemish Primitive painters, had actively aspired to be. (It was this Philip who has come down in history as the man who captured Joan of Arc and sold her to the English to be burnt.) In the end he had acknowledged the suzerainty of the French king. This did not mean that his son renounced all dreams of grandeur. On the contrary, as effective regent during the last two years of his father's lifetime, Charles fought the French, won initial victories, recovered certain lands previously surrendered by his father, and obtained the French king's daughter for his first wife.

It was his daughter Marie by his third wife, Margaret of York, sister of Edward IV of England, who was to be married to Maximilian. Charles of Burgundy had already intrigued among the Germans to get himself nominated as a future Emperor; when this came to nothing he began to concentrate on getting Burgundy raised from a duchy to a kingdom. This was entirely a matter for the Emperor of the day. He alone could make a new king: it was one of the few unassailable powers still vested in him. Charles of Burgundy was far more powerful as a ruler than Frederick of Austria; he was almost infinitely richer. But with all his power and with all the pomp and glitter of the Burgundian court, with its marvellous pictures and tapestries of the Flemish school, its golden artefacts, its superb armoury, the dazzling richness of its costumes, he still had to kneel to a penniless and unsuccessful Emperor, whose sole material assets, the silver and copper mines of the Tyrol, were mortgaged to the Fuggers of Augsburg, then well embarked on the astonishing career which was to make them the bankers of Europe and the sinews of Habsburg power.

From the Fuggers the Emperor now borrowed enough to take him to meet the Duke of Burgundy at Trier for the betrothal of his son. It was a fabulous occasion. Charles had transported to Trier in a great convoy of waggons an appreciable part of the whole Burgundian treasure from Brussels, Bruges and Ghent. The Emperor had himself, only his natural dignity, which was considerable, and the immensely personable fourteen-year-old Maximilian, who won all hearts, including Marie's. Negotiations were soon under way, against a background of ostentatious revelry and feasting, and things were going swimmingly. Charles was taking the final conclusion so much for granted that he had put in train arrangements for his coronation as King of Burgundy and had actually ordered his new crown. Then suddenly, without warning, Frederick broke off the conversations and went back to Austria leaving everything hanging in the air – either because Charles had pushed his claim too hard, or because Frederick had heard disquieting news, or rumours, about Burgundian intrigues with the enemies of Habsburg. It looked like the end of Frederick's particular dream; but in fact it was the end of Charles.

Charles was furious and, in his rage, embarked on a course of conquest, designed first to link up his territories in the south with his rich lands in the north. He failed. In one battle after another his army was shattered by the French under Louis XI, the 'Universal Spider', astute, cold-blooded, tough and very cunning. One

27

of the strangest episodes of this struggle, romanticized in Sir Walter Scott's *Quentin Durward*, was when Charles held his great enemy captive at Péronne and let him go free. In the end Charles, at forty-four, was killed in his last battle near Nancy in 1477. His body, left lying on the field, was gnawed by wolves. By then, in his desperation, he had already agreed unconditionally to Marie's betrothal to Maximilian, in order to win Imperial support. But with his death came the end of Burgundy's existence as an independent power; and with this came also the foundation of Habsburg might, and the beginning of the great struggle between Austria and France which was to dominate the European scene for centuries to come and secure that continental balance which made it possible for England to achieve her empire.

Even so, for a moment after Charles's death it looked as though the betrothal could never end in marriage. Louis and France had triumphed. Louis would take all Burgundy. Above all he would take the young princess under his protection and marry her to the Dauphin, Charles, then only nine. It was only Marie's determined effort of will and the skilful and resolute manoeuvring of her mother, Margaret of York, which won the day. The Flemings, who were awkward subjects, forever scheming for their independence, might have no love for the dukes of Burgundy, but they certainly had no desire to be swallowed up by France. Without prejudice to future plans, for the time being they backed their young princess – and Maximilian. The marriage took place. Habsburg came into a dazzling inheritance. But Habsburg also inherited the hostility of France.

Thus a most decisive moment in the development of Europe, and a highly prophetic one, was the first battle of Guinegatte, a village in the Pas de Calais at the other end of Europe from Vienna, in which the young Maximilian defeated the French in his first test of arms in 1479. Guinegatte was to be doubly prophetic. It was here again, in 1513, towards the end of his life, that Maximilian in person fought under the young King of England, Henry VIII, in what came to be known as the Battle of the Spurs, because the French cavalry fled at full gallop, spurring their horses to be away. That was part of a little war, irrelevant for England but an integral part of the developing Franco-Austrian pattern, that settled nothing. It marked the opening of the remarkable and mutually suspicious partnership between Austria and England which was to reach its apotheosis in the War of the Spanish Succession with the great victories of Marlborough and Prince Eugene.

Maximilian had to fight for Burgundy against France. He had to fight for his own position against his subjects in the Netherlands: there was to be a time, indeed, when he was held prisoner by his own subjects in Bruges. He fought elsewhere as well, conducting a badly-thought-out invasion of Italy, for example, and moving across to Vienna at his father's request after the death of Matthew Corvinus in 1490 to drive the Hungarians out of the Habsburg lands. But although he was perpetually fighting he was not a great warrior prince. He was brave enough, but generalship did not come naturally to him. His wars were either hurried reactions to aggression or the threat of it, or by-products of the innumerable schemes for securing the Habsburg position that followed each other in a very fertile imagination so fast that they tripped over one another: his impetuous career left a long trail marked by the debris of unfulfilled designs. He enjoyed the pleasures of life too much and was too inconstant in his resolution (though hard and tough enough in a crisis) to embark on a long and carefully calculated plan of military aggrandizement of the kind required to establish him firmly and unassailably as the dominant power in central Europe.

Besides this he had no money: like his father before him and his magnificent grandson in years to come, he depended on the Augsburg Fuggers and Welsers, who would help him when it suited them – when, that is to say, he was needed to protect their properties and investments and long-range financial plans. But there was no money to spare to buy the support of the German princes for operations which would benefit Habsburg alone – for example, a hopeful scheme to capture Brittany. In the intervals between his wars, first at his rich Burgundian court, then, later, at Innsbruck which he turned into his capital, Maximilian hunted and jousted. He also made his court famous for poetry and music. For example, it was he who established the choir which came to be known as the Vienna Singing Boys, and, much later, was to nourish Haydn and

Schubert in their time, surviving the fall of the monarchy down to the present day. He cultivated scholars and philosophers. He evidently prided himself on being all things to all men, holding his own among his rough fighting men, meeting his knights on their own ground in innumerable tournaments, joining in their barrack-room horse-play – and then snubbing them by exalting above them, with the most flattering attentions, a painter or a versifier. He was sympathetic to the young Martin Luther, then in the process of making his own name – even though that importunate and clamant monk took as his special target of abuse in the matter of the sale of indulgences the Archbishop of Mainz, whose support as one of the seven Electors Maximilian urgently needed to secure the succession for his grandson. Luther admired him and left written down many of the famous anecdotes which showed the Emperor in the light he most preferred. For example, one of the Emperor's companions, puzzled by a sudden outburst of laughter, asked him what was so funny. 'I was thinking,' he replied, 'how odd that God had so ordained the spiritual and temporal realms as to place the first under the rule of a drunken and dissolute Pope, the second under a hunter of chamois.'

But below all this ebullient and often self-contradictory activity, Maximilian had two qualities inherited from his father. In private he would dream, and one of his most remarkable fantasies, confided to his daughter, Margaret, after the death of his second wife, was to make himself Pope as well as Emperor, and thus unite all Christendom under one supreme head: 'And not finding it for any reason good that we should marry again, we have resolved never again to lie beside a naked woman. And we are sending tomorrow to Rome to the Pope to find a way . . . to accept us as coadjutator, so that after his death we can be assured of the Papacy, becoming a priest and after that a saint, so that after our death you will have to adore me.' All he needed was a certain sum in cash to bribe the cardinals. He signed this letter, 'from the hand of your good father, Maximilian, future Pope'.

It was no wonder that he was hard to understand, that his contemporaries left so many contradictory accounts of his nature, not knowing when to take him seriously, when not. Perhaps he hardly knew himself. He was a ruler who would have fitted very well into an established pattern of power; but no such pattern then existed. He was a man who needed a horizon: he lacked the consistency, as well as the means, to impose his own horizon, first on his own mind, which raced too often like a ship's screws out of the water in a storm, then on his environment. There was, however, one critical particular in which he showed himself possessed of all the Habsburg tenacity of purpose.

He saw that the future of his house lay in the marriages of his children and his grandchildren. According to legend it was Matthew Corvinus, the Hungarian king, who composed the celebrated couplet:

> *Bella gerant fortes: tu, felix Austria, nube:*
> *Nam quae Mars aliis, dat tibi regna Venus.**

If so, he was thinking in the main of the Burgundian marriage. But it was Maximilian, fighter that he was, who turned out to be the greatest marriage-broker in a period when to achieve a well-considered marriage was the main preoccupation of princely diplomacy. Even he, however, could not foresee the magnitude of the consequences of the first of his great transactions.

Marie of Burgundy had two children, Philip and Margaret. She was only twenty-five when she died. Her horse threw her and fell with her when, together with her husband, she was flying her falcon at a heron in the marshlands outside Bruges. Maximilian was deeply affected. He could also have been ruined. Ghent and Bruges rose against him. They were tired of the expenses and uncertainties of the constant war with France. They were tired of the Emperor's German mercenaries. They were rich and proud. Marie had left them an infant prince whom they could bring up to rule over them. They quickly came to an agreement with the French king: France could keep all the disputed lands now under her occupation; further, Maximilian's infant daughter, Margaret, was delivered over to France as the prospective bride of the Dauphin, taking more of Burgundy as her dowry. But this was going too far. The other Burgundian provinces had other views. They fell in behind Maximilian and supplied him with the means to suppress

* The strong make war; thou, happy Austria, marry:
  What Mars grants others, Venus gives to thee.

the rebellion. Maximilian got hold of his son Philip and put him under the care of his grandmother, Margaret of York, who was to bring him up at Malines. Philip's sister Margaret, however, was already gone, apparently beyond recall. Spirited off to France, she was brought up in the great castle of Amboise on the Loire in the style befitting a future Queen of France. In fact she was never to be a queen; but she had a long and varied life ahead of her.

All this took place in 1482. Three years later, with Maximilian immersed in Burgundian affairs, came the final blow to Frederick in Vienna, the invasion of his country and the occupation of his capital by the Hungarian king. Something had to be done quickly to ensure the very survival of Habsburg; the German princes were calling for a new Emperor to show enterprise and resolution, to be everything that Frederick was not. Frederick was nearing seventy, Maximilian, only twenty-six, still a youth in his eyes. But if the succession was to be assured, now was the time to act. The old man who should have been broken was still wonderfully serene. 'To forget what cannot be recovered is the supreme felicity,' was one of his favourite sayings, and he had lived up to it. But, under the spur of absolute necessity, he could still act. He now decided to have his son crowned King of the Romans, which meant his eventual succession as Emperor. Father and son met for the first time in eight years, for the first time since Maximilian had set off to Flanders for his wedding to poor Marie. The formal election took place smoothly at Frankfurt, in spite of the attempts of the new French king, Charles VIII, to bribe the Electors. The coronation followed at Aix-la-Chapelle, the young Maximilian seated in splendour on Charlemagne's ancient throne.

Even now he had trouble on his hands. Returning to Flanders after the tremendous round of coronation celebrations, he found the citizenry up in arms again. This time it was the turn of Bruges, where he was seized and put under house arrest and held prisoner for four months. The Electors fulminated, the Pope threatened the entire city with excommunication, and Ferdinand and Isabella of Spain prepared a fleet to rescue him. It was a remarkable situation when the Emperor elect could be held prisoner in this way. But Bruges at this time was the richest and most magnificent city in Europe, the proudest too, with a population of at least 100,000, twice the size of Brussels, and the centre not only of the textile industry but also of Western-European finance. 'There are hundreds here,' wrote the young bride of Philip the Fair, in the fourteenth century, 'who have more the air of queens than myself'. It was at Bruges, in 1429, that Philip the Good had founded the Order of the Golden Fleece to celebrate his marriage with Isabella of Portugal, and one of Maximilian's first acts after the death of Charles the Rash was to make himself Grand Master of this Order, which had its chapters in Bruges Cathedral. In a word, although the grandeur of the city was on the decline, largely because of the silting up of the Zwyn, so that commerce was shifting to Antwerp, it was still far more than a city. As far as riches and dignity went it was a kingdom in itself. As such it forced Maximilian to declare that he would abide by his agreement with the French at the Treaty of Arras (1482), and at last allowed him to go free. But then, with an astonishing burst of energy, the seventy-year-old Frederick marched into Burgundy at the head of a formidable imperial army, forcing Bruges and Ghent to submit and releasing Maximilian from the promise obtained under duress.

There was one more humiliation. Some time later, while Matthew Corvinus still ruled over Austria from the Hofburg in Vienna and Frederick gave himself up entirely to his dreams, his quasi-scientific studies, his alchemy, in Linz, Maximilian, determined to marry again, contrived to betroth himself to Anne of Brittany, heiress to the remote Atlantic duchy which had still managed to keep the French king at bay. This precipitated the final act of a ludicrous comedy hard to match in the history of dynastic marriages. In the first act, by marrying Marie of Burgundy, Maximilian had defeated the designs of Louis XI to secure her as the bride of the Dauphin Charles, then only nine, and ten years younger than poor Marie. The next act had been the seizure and sequestration of the dead Marie's daughter, Margaret, who was still, at Amboise, the French queen designate. Louis had died meanwhile, and now, faced with the prospect of Brittany falling to Habsburg, the Dauphin's elder sister, who was acting regent of France, sent her brother off to capture for himself the fifteen-year-old duchess in her castle at Rennes. It was on this occasion that the German princes refused to vote supplies and troops for

Maximilian to march to the rescue of his betrothed. Anne had to submit and, to make sure of Brittany, the Dauphin married her at once, leaving Margaret to be returned to her father as not wanted after all. She was a girl of great spirit and humour. Later she was to marry John of Spain, and it was on her way to her new home that a great storm arose and it seemed that her ship would go down with everyone in it. Margaret was not dismayed. Instead of lamenting, she composed an elegant little couplet and slipped the folded paper into a locket which she carried on her bracelet:

Ci-gît Margot, la gente demoiselle,
*Qu'eux deux maris, et si mourut pucelle.**

In the end, perhaps a little sick of dealings with princes, Maximilian decided to go for cash instead of territory. Probably, when his father at last died in 1493, he was shocked to find that the treasury really was empty. At any rate, to raise some money quickly he took one of those eccentric plunges which characterized his whole career. This Emperor, this scion of ancient lineage, this knightly master of the highest order of chivalry, scandalized Europe by marring Bianca Sforza, daughter of the Duke of Milan, whose grandfather, successor to the Viscontis, had been a peasant-born soldier of fortune. It was the last time for four hundred years that a Habsburg, other than an errant younger son, was to marry outside the most restricted princely circles. It should have been worth it: Bianca brought with her three hundred thousand golden ducats and another hundred thousand worth of jewels and clothes, gold and silver plate and household goods (her chamber-pot was silver; her embroidery needles were gold). All were transported to Innsbruck on mules across the Brenner Pass in the winter snows. But Bianca, as befitted the daughter of a *parvenu* despot (who, nevertheless, was a great patron of the arts: Leonardo da Vinci was called in to design and supervise the decorations for the proxy wedding in Milan), was hopelessly extravagant. Maximilian was not businessman enough to tie her dowry up. Between them, but separately, they got through it in no time at all – separately be-

* Here lies Margot, the noble lady,
  Who had two husbands but died a maid.

cause Maximilian never took to Bianca, who spent even more than he did, and in the most ridiculous ways. She had no children. So her husband had to think long and hard about his own children who were now his only assets.

In 1495, with the aim of encircling a France which under the new king, Charles VIII, was becoming more aggressive, the new Emperor entered into a solemn alliance with Spain; and to seal that alliance he pledged his son Philip and his daughter Margaret (back in Malines for her eight years as prospective queen of France) to the two younger children of Ferdinand and Isabella, Joanna and John. It was a solemn pledge, offered with all form in the great church of St. Gudule at Brussels. It was to lead to the summit of Habsburg glory.

Spain at this time was emerging as a major power. In 1469 Isabella of Castile and Léon had married Ferdinand of Aragon. Five years later she succeeded to the throne of Castile and León, and in 1479 Ferdinand succeeded to Aragon. The Moors in the south were steadily pushed back, and in 1492, with the fall of Granada, all Spain was united under one family. Freed thus of their main burden and preoccupation Ferdinand and Isabella immediately turned their minds to other things. And in that same year they fitted out Columbus for his first voyage of discovery; he had been importuning them for a long time past, but the struggle with the Moors and the extirpation of heresy and the forcible conversion of the Jews at home had filled their minds to the exclusion of all else. Discovery was in the air. The Portuguese sailors, urged on by Henry the Navigator, had been exploring the coast of Africa and had established themselves in the Azores. Columbus, the Genoese, had approached not only the Spanish monarchs, but also Henry VII of England and Maximilian's enemy, Charles VIII of France – in vain. That he ultimately got Spain to back him was one of those stupendous accidents which change the history of the world and make nonsense of comfortable assumptions that everything that happens is bound to happen as it does. Mexico and Peru would have sooner or later fallen to the Old World: they could well have escaped conquest in the fanatically bloody-minded Spanish manner and the imposition of Spanish Catholicism. Nearer home, the treasure of the New World was for two hundred years to build up and sustain the arms of Spain and help turn her into the grandest and most feared European power.

The Spain into which Maximilian married his children did not look like that at all. The marriages took place in 1496 while Columbus was still engaged on his voyages of exploration. Twenty years were to pass before Cortes arrived in Mexico, nearly forty before Pizarro burst in upon Peru. By that time Spain was Habsburg: Maximilian's grandson, Charles, succeeded to the Spanish throne in 1516. Maximilian lived just long enough to see this happen and to know that on his death Charles would be Emperor and master of half Europe.

It took more accidents to make this happen. Maximilian's son Philip was a handsome and talented youth with a mind of his own. Even when he came of age officially, at sixteen, and was thus in his own right ruler of Burgundy, he was quarrelling with his father and refusing to allow him to embroil Burgundy in his endless struggle with France. But the quarrel was surmounted and Philip settled down with his Spanish bride Joanna. It was a difficult marriage. Philip was gay, extrovert and something of a womanizer. Joanna, with the taint of madness in her family, combined a brooding religious fanaticism with an overpowering sensuality. Her husband's body became an object of devotion. It was soon too much for the unfortunate Philip, who could only control her jealous rages by refusing to share her bed. Her brother, John, was also over-sexed. So much so that when he met Margaret, his bride, safely arrived after her perilous sea-voyage, he could not keep away from her. Isabella, his mother, was so perturbed that she urged her new daughter-in-law to hold herself back from her husband, who, she feared, was on the way to wearing himself out. Sex, she feared, might be the death of him. And, indeed, the young heir did die after only eighteen months of marriage. That left his elder sister as heir to the throne. But in no time at all she too was dead, and, almost at once, her infant son. Thus it was that the younger sister, Joanna, Duchess of Burgundy, Philip's disastrous wife, was now heiress to all Spain. She already had three children, two girls and the infant Charles; she was to have more. It was now very much on the cards that Charles would be king of Spain. But a good deal still depended on luck: if Isabella died first, Ferdinand might marry again and produce a new heir. Isabella indeed did die first, but the Habsburg luck held.

She died in 1504. Long before then she knew that Joanna would never be fit to succeed her. She had been appalled by her daughter's condition when she had returned to Spain with Philip in 1501 to swear her oath to the Cortes, or Parliament, as heiress apparent. Philip had gone back to the Netherlands and left her in Spain, where she soon showed every sign of madness. When at last she followed her husband back to Brussels she behaved with such violence, murderously attacking his current mistress, that she had to be locked in her apartments. She had still another child by Philip, all the same. Now, furious that his mother-in-law had excluded Joanna and left the regency to Ferdinand, Philip and Joanna hurried off to Madrid to protest and claim their own. Already, with extreme expedition, Ferdinand had remarried. His new wife, Germaine de Foix, was young and pretty. The situation looked very dangerous indeed. But Philip won over the Cortes. Ferdinand resigned the regency and set off with his new bride for Naples.

Then it was Philip's turn to die, the last of an extraordinary run of dynastic fatalities. Some said he had been poisoned by Joanna in a fit of jealousy; others that Ferdinand had poisoned him. Be that as it may, Ferdinand returned from Naples to resume the regency, and Joanna became permanently unhinged. She had been told of a prince who had come to life after fourteen years in the grave. Confined by Ferdinand, she watched over Philip's open coffin for fourteen years. During all this time her first four children, the future Charles V among them, were being brought up in Malines by Margaret, their aunt, once putative Queen of France, then wife to the heir of Spain, married again to Prince Philibert of Savoy, quickly widowed for the second time, then appointed by her father, Maximilian, to be regent of the Netherlands in 1509, which she managed very well. Once upon a time the painter Memling had painted Margaret in bridal magnificence as St. Catherine in his wonderful 'Mystic Wedding', with her grandmother Margaret of York, in mourning, as St. Barbara. Now Margaret of Burgundy wore the widow's clothes, and she was bringing up the future King of Spain and Emperor. More than that; she was responsible also for a future Queen of Denmark, a future Queen of Portugal, and most importantly, a future Queen of Hungary.

The Hungarian marriage was Maximilian's most imperative and difficult operation in this field, its consequences reaching down into the twentieth century. In 1491, when Maximilian had pushed the Hungarians out of Austria after the death of Matthew Corvinus, he had signed a treaty with the new king, Ladislaus, which stipulated that if there was no male heir the Hungarian crown would go to Habsburg.

When the time came it was touch and go. The Hungarian nobility, strong in their constitutional powers, had other ideas. But Maximilian won through – at one stage formally betrothing his infant grand-daughter Mary to an unborn child before its sex was known. This turned out to be the future heir, Prince Louis, whose premature birth, not surprising in the circumstances, killed his mother: the minute child was kept warm and alive by being plunged into the opened bodies of freshly killed animals. In the end Maximilian got his way. The double marriage contract was signed in 1506; Prince Louis was to marry Maximilian's grand-daughter Mary; Princess Ann one of Maximilian's grandsons, either Charles or Ferdinand. Even then there were many difficulties to be overcome. Maximilian was still desperately short of cash. Then he fell ill. Finally he could not produce the promised bride-groom for Princess Ann: his grandson Charles had already been promised elsewhere (he was betrothed to half the princesses of Europe before he finally married Isabella of Portugal); Charles's younger brother Ferdinand, born in Spain, had been brought up at the Spanish court, and his maternal grandfather Ferdinand of Aragon was determined to keep him in Spain to succeed him when he died. In the end an extraordinary deal was made. Maximilian himself, nearing sixty, solemnly undertook to marry the twelve-year-old Hungarian princess if neither of his grandsons, Charles or Ferdinand, came forward to claim her within a year. Thus it was he, the Emperor, who knelt in betrothal to the girl princess in St. Stephen's Cathedral in Vienna. At the same ceremony, the two nine-year-olds, Louis of Hungary and Mary of Austria, exchanged their solemn pledges.

As things turned out, Ferdinand of Aragon was dead within the year. His grandson and namesake could now, if he chose, marry the Hungarian princess. He chose to do so. And in so doing laid the firm foundation for the rise of the House of Austria.

It was the Fuggers who paid for all this. Maximilian already owed them a fortune, but they still needed the Emperor. Their immediate concern was to get control of the silver mines of Hungary, the output from which was depressing the prices obtained from the mines in the Tyrol. But they were so rich now that they needed status more than further millions. There were three brothers, grandsons of the original Augsburg weaver: Maximilian ennobled them all. They were ardent Catholics, fierce and damaging opponents of Luther and the Reformation. Besides their personal loans to the Habsburgs, they heavily financed Maximilian in the abortive campaign against Venice at the request of Pope Julius II. After Maximilian's death, they and they alone made it possible for Charles to carry on his tense struggle for the Imperial crown in the teeth of the fantastic bribes of the French king. Without the Fuggers, it is almost certainly true to say, the Habsburgs could never have emerged from the Middle Ages as a major power. The activities of this remarkable family carried them into every corner of European commerce and finance. Their imagination, allied with shrewdness, was unlimited. Their wealth was past computing. They were the king-makers. When Charles, as Emperor, attended the famous Diet of Augsburg in 1530 he stayed in a Fugger house, and it was on this occasion that Antonius Fugger is said to have used an Imperial bond to light a little fire of cinnamon before the Emperor's startled and gratified eyes. On a later occasion Charles was being proudly shown the accumulated treasure of the French king: 'There is a weaver in Augsburg,' he said, 'who could buy all that and more besides out of his own purse.'

Maximilian died at sixty, moneyless as he had lived, splendid to the view as he had been all his life. He was given an elaborately splendid monument at Innsbruck among the mountains he loved above all other homes. He had been kept young by the two child brides, his grand-daughters, who had come to live with him while they grew up. His heart he had carried to Bruges to rest in the tomb of his own first wife, Marie of Burgundy, dead now for more than thirty years. He left, without at all understanding it, an Austria which was to be shaped through the centuries by two major forces: the challenge of France in the West and of the young Ottoman Empire in the East. The Turks had taken Constantinople in 1453 and were now threatening the commerce of Venice, of Italy itself, on the one hand, and on the other, were pushing stubbornly and effectively through the Balkans and up the Danube to Vienna. There was another force which just touched the Emperor's last years: the force of the Reformation. More remote in its effects, which would one day be formidable indeed, was the emergence of Muscovy from the Tatar yoke, with Ivan III's great victory in 1480. Nobody knew anything about Russia, but Maximilian, ever on the look-out for new allies, had heard enough to know that Ivan was a prince to be reckoned with. Before he died the first embassies were exchanged between the last medieval Emperor and the first Russian Tsar.

3

Habsburg over Europe:
Charles V and Martin Luther

CHARLES was nineteen when his grandfather died at Innsbruck. He was vulnerable and diffident, in no way a scholar, keen on hunting, late developing, but blessed with a good enough mind to grasp fairly quickly both the essentials and the subtleties of statesmanship and diplomacy. He was a man who could recognize his own mistakes, and he did this all his life, even though the lessons he drew from them were sometimes the wrong lessons. He was one of the most remarkable rulers who had ever lived; but his whole career was to demonstrate the limitations which hedge in even the most gifted and nominally powerful who are not also unscrupulous egotists of an essentially destructive kind. His grandfather, Maximilian, had sought to consolidate Habsburg dynastic power within the medieval framework, which was falling to pieces. Charles, inheriting vast territories, backed in the first instance by the Fuggers, started poor as his grandfather had died, but as time went on he commanded undreamt-of wealth, not only the treasure of the Americas, but also the riches of the Netherlands: for although Bruges and Ghent had passed the summit of their glory, Antwerp and Brussels were now ascendant, and the Low Countries as a whole were bringing industry and commerce to a peak never before known in the history of Europe.

Charles, in a word, was destined to preside over the fashioning of the modern world. In 1619, the first year of his long reign, Magellan was engaged on the astonishing circumnavigation of the globe which killed him, while Cortes had embarked on the conquest of Mexico. It was indeed, for a spell, possible to dream again of the one world, of Charlemagne's one world, extended now across the oceans. There was to be a moment when Charles

41

could almost believe that he was succeeding in establishing a unitary and global Christendom. He failed. The story of his life may be seen as the failure of the richest and most powerful man in the world to impose an international religious and secular order. The story of the modern world may be seen in terms of the consequences of that failure, punctuated by attempts on the part of inferior individuals to succeed where Charles failed. The consequence which concerns us here is the development of the Central-European Habsburg complex as one powerful and embattled realm among others.

The upbringing of the young Charles, thin-faced, the Habsburg jaw so marked that it impeded his speech and made his mouth hang open (later he grew a most becoming beard), but wiry and tough with a well-made body and long, straight legs, was daunting. He was six when his father, Philip, died, leaving him the Burgundian inheritance. His mother, Joanna, lived on in Spain. At ten, the centre of a miniature but very rich court in Brussels, he was assisting in the Council of State. Thus it was that he came to rely too much on his governor, the Sieur de Chièvres, and his senior tutor, who was later to be Pope Adrian VI. He was seventeen when it was decided to send him from Flanders to Spain to claim his inheritance. He voyaged with his favourite sister, Eleanor, who was to be Queen of Portugal. Because of dangerous seas, brother and sister had themselves put ashore where they first sighted land, on the wild coast of Asturias, leaving the rest of the escorting fleet to sail on. It took them two months of exhausting and sometimes hazardous journeying to reach Valladolid across the mountains. It was a suitable introduction to a lifetime of travel, slow and laborious travel over unmade roads, dizzy mountain passes, perilous fords. Immensely tough as he was, in the end this journeying wore him down. He was to be the most travelled monarch in history.

This first journey at seventeen was very much a testing time. Charles had to encounter first his mother, dragging out her days in physical squalor and mental ruin, then his younger brother, Ferdinand, whom he had never met, amiable, highly presentable, wholly Spanish in upbringing and outlook. There was strong feeling among Spaniards that Ferdinand should be their future ruler rather than the unknown and foreign prince from the North.

But Ferdinand had an easy, open and friendly disposition. He was still only fourteen, but his head was not in the least turned by the Spanish flatterers among whom he had grown up, by the splendour with which he was surrounded, by the knowledge that his maternal grandfather, Isabella's Ferdinand, thought of him as the heir to all Spain, by the fact that wherever he went the popular demonstrations in his favour were in marked contrast to the reserve with which his elder brother was received. He seemed to lack all ambition for himself. Considering his deplorable upbringing, first trailing round as a child with his lunatic mother and sharing for a time her sequestration in the squalor of Tordesillas, then elevated by his grandfather, it was remarkable that already he was imbued with that Habsburg sense of apartness, of being chosen, so that it was unthinkable for him to ally himself with any faction against the elder brother whom he had never met, but who was indisputably the head of the house to which he, Ferdinand, belonged and which was set above all others. For all his cheeerful and unassuming nature, Ferdinand had an explosive temper, which went with his reddish hair, and he could be, on occasion, as stubborn as any Habsburg. But it was not until after many years of amicable co-existence that he began to assert himself against his brother and finally met him head-on in a bitter quarrel about the succession to the Imperial Crown. Even then, Ferdinand was not fighting for himself but for his son Maximilian, against Charles's son Philip.

For a long time all went well. Charles went out of his way to treat his young brother as his equal and his confidant. By their own bearing both the young prices rendered null the malicious squabbling and intrigue and counter-intrigue between Charles's showy and arrogant Burgundian retinue and the grandees of the Spanish court. But it was soon clear to Charles that if he were to take hold of Spain and establish his position there, Ferdinand must be removed from the scene. More than this, he already saw that he would one day need a deputy to take up residence in Austria and weld the central European possessions of the Habsburgs into some sort of shape. So in no time at all the eager boy was sent off to the

43

Netherlands, first to establish himself in Brussels and then to learn something of life outside Spain.

It was a year after this that the old Emperor, grandfather Maximilian, died at Innsbruck and the great struggle for the Imperial crown began in earnest. Maximilian died in the belief that the promises he had bought from the Electors, always for stiff prices, would secure the almost automatic succession of his grandson. He should have known better. There had been a radical change in Europe since the time of his own election. France and Spain had crystallized into great nation states. England, under Henry VIII, with Cardinal Wolsey at his elbow, sought to hold the balance between France and Spain and thus play a decisive role as the arbiter of Europe. Gone were the days when a moneyless Habsburg could hope to manoeuvre the seven Electors into sustaining his claims to the Imperial crown. Francis I of France, deeply apprehensive of the growing power of Spain, decided that at all costs the Habsburgs must be weakened. He put himself up for election as an elementary move in the new great power game. Wolsey, who was determined to be pope one day, saw no reason why his master, Henry VIII, should not become Emperor himself if a deadlock could be contrived between Francis and Charles. There were lesser candidates, who hoped they might be chosen if the Electors decided that they would prefer, as often in the past, a nominal head of the Empire who would be more easily manageable than any of the new giants; King Louis of Hungary and his uncle, King Sigismund of Poland, were both in the lists.

But the real fight was between Francis and Charles. Francis was rich, and he had behind him also the immense fortune of his mother, Louise of Savoy. Charles was poor; but he was backed by the Fuggers. For a time it looked as though it would be a straight fight with money. Francis's bribes were stupendous. He made it quite clear that he would, as he could, outbid Charles at every point. The Pope himself, the Medici Leo X, the patron of Raphael, who spent vast sums on letters and the arts while neglecting his pastoral duties so blatantly that the Papacy was never to recover its lost authority, quite cynically observed that the crown was up for auction and would go to the highest bidder. In fact it did not work out like that. Certainly without the Fuggers, and without the drive and determination and organizing ability of Charles's remarkable aunt, Maximilian's daughter Margaret, Regent of the Netherlands, Charles could not have stayed in the contest at all. But the final deciding factor was something that neither the French nor the English, nor perhaps even Charles himself, had taken into account: the hero worship of the German peoples for Maximilian, their dead Emperor, and their resentment at the pretensions of the French. Frederick of Saxony, who had not only refused to stand for election (he thought, correctly, that a strong Emperor was needed to unite Europe against the menace of Islam), but had also scorned all bribes, formed a rallying point for an uprush of public opinion which caused even the greediest of the Electors, Brandenburg, who had been promised by Francis the governorship of Germany and a heavily dowered French princess as his bride, to think twice. So that even when the Pope threw his weight behind Francis it did not avail. The Germans chose their own Emperor, and all the intrigue, the bribes, the intimidation went for nothing. Charles was triumphantly elected by a unanimous vote.

He was twenty-one, and he entered into his exalted vocation with a high, religious seriousness. He was very much a Habsburg, which meant that he had his full share of Habsburg possessiveness. But, unlike any other monarch of the day, he also embodied a revival of the dream of a united Christendom in the fulfilment of which he was ready to sacrifice himself.

It was too late. In 1517 Martin Luther had nailed his ninety-five theses to the church-door at Wittenberg; and since then his following had been growing all over Germany, immensely accelerated by Pope Leo's cynical and lazy toleration of infinite corruption. When Charles came to be crowned King of the Romans at Aix-la-Chapelle in 1521, things had gone so far that the papacy had to summon all its power to put Luther down. The young Emperor's first great task after his coronation was to ride up the Rhine to Worms, refulgent with all the brilliance and panoply of secular power, for a personal confrontation, at the famous Diet of Worms, with this monk who was in the process of shattering for ever the pretensions of both Pope and Emperor to speak and act for all Christians everywhere. Roughly ten years after the election in which he himself had half-heartedly contended, Henry VIII of England was himself to defy the Pope in order to divorce Catherine, the daughter of Ferdinand and Isabella of Spain, the young Emperor's aunt, and, destroying Wolsey in the process, take England out of the Catholic community of peoples. Ten years later, too, the Christian King of France was to ally himself with a conquering Moslem potentate, Suleiman the Magnificent, in his triumphant drive to the walls of Vienna and beyond. This was the first statement of a recurring theme to sound out loudly over and over again for the next two hundred years. Everybody knows that in so far as a dynasty may be said to have a mission, the Habsburg mission for two hundred years was to stand between Western Europe and the devouring Turks. Nearly everyone forgets that France, so proudly presented as the flower of civilization, for two hundred years egged on and assisted the Turks in their repeated efforts to overrun and destroy the Habsburg bastion.

Charles was to be made very acutely aware of the disintegration of Christendom during the course of his long and laborious reign. And it was this awareness, bringing with it a crushing sense of personal defeat, which was the root cause of his abdication after more than thirty years of unremitting struggle. He was Emperor. He was powerful enough to nominate his own successor. He was the most august figure of his age and he ruled over an *imperium* dazzling in its vastness, its range, its swiftly growing riches. All this was not enough. The young Emperor had set out fom his coronation to meet Luther, dedicated to the task of unifying and purifying Christendom. In this task he had failed. It was still a fine and noble thing that he had raised his family to the heights of secular power and worldly splendour. He had thus done his duty by that family, and he was glad to see it prosper. But, at fifty-six, he wanted no more part in it.

To his medieval dream he applied the mind and manners of a modern man. The great Titian portrait is all wisdom, experience hard won, disillusion tempered by irony and humour, half-amused, half-contemptuous tolerance of past extravagance and pretensions. To see him as he faced Luther and put the Imperial ban on him, captured the French king and kept him in prison for eight months, harried the Pope and humbled him to the dust, it is better to look at Holbein's portrait painted twenty years earlier.

There is no suffering in that face, only alertness and watchfulness developed to an extraordinary degree. The round, almost bullet head with its short hair-cut, in conjunction with the long predatory nose and the harsh angularity of the jaw and chin suggest clearly enough the element of imperious violence, indeed cruelty, which was to come out in his treatment of his enemies. But behind this watchfulness and ruthlessness the eyes are also withdrawn and dreaming. These two masterpieces, images of the most powerful figure of the seventeenth century early and late in his reign, form a marvellous commentary on the limitations and the vanity of human pretensions – on its heroism too. For the mildly sardonic potentate of the Titian portrait had suffered much. He was still only forty-eight. He was tormented by gout. He had every excuse for bitterness against his enemies and for vain glory in his own achievements. For he had just won his crushing victory at Mühlberg against the Protestant forces, the League of Schmalkalden, and believed that he had settled the religious quarrel for ever. Seven years later he gave up.

When the young Charles faced Luther across the table at Worms in 1521, he was not sustained by fanaticism of any kind. He knew as well as anybody that Rome stood in most urgent need of reform and that Pope Leo X who, in Raphael's portrait, is as close to us today as he was to Luther and Charles, had hopelessly discredited an already rotten institution. Charles had observed Luther's progress to Rome to stand up to the Pope in person, his triumphal return, his public burning of the Papal Bull of excommunication. He could sympathize with the best of those who idolized this stiff-necked rebel for defying a corrupt, an extortionate, a foreign authority. But he, Charles V, was also authority embodied. He would have been ready, he would have been eager, to assist in the convening of a council which would examine the condition of the Church and propose radical reforms. He would have agreed that Christianity was best served not by purchasing indulgences or even by leaving all the problems of conduct in the hands of priestly confessors, but, rather, by obedience to the dictates of the private conscience. To question publicly the very foundation of the Church and to deny it all authority was, however, quite another

47

matter. So Charles spoke, not leaving the matter to be arranged by Papal officials, but in person, in all his anointed majesty:

I am descended from a long line of Christian Emperors of this noble German nation, and of the Catholic kings of Spain, the archdukes of Austria and the dukes of Burgundy. All were faithful to the death to the Church of Rome, and they defended the Catholic Church and the honour of God.

I have resolved to follow in their steps. A single monk who goes counter to all Christianity for a thousand years must be wrong. Therefore I am resolved to stake my lands, my friends, my body, my blood, my life and my soul in pledge for this cause.

The single monk was placed formally under the ban of Empire. Henceforth he was outside the law and any man might kill him with impunity. Defiantly he trundled off from Worms in his famous two-wheeled cart. Almost at once he was seized by men sent by his great admirer, the Elector of Saxony, and carried off for safety to the strong fortress castle of the Wartburg in Thuringia. It had been Frederick of Saxony who had stood most faithfully by Charles, refusing to be bribed, in the bitter electoral contest less than two years before. Now this incorruptible old man went into opposition, formalizing the existence of the religious schism which was to convulse Europe for more than a hundred years, destroying much of it in the process, and always with a Habsburg as the chief champion of Rome.

It was never to be a straight fight. Charles trying to stem the Reformation, his grand-nephew Ferdinand II presiding over the Counter-Reformation and the Thirty Years War, ardently as they fought for the true faith, were pushed every way by dynastic conflicts and crises which so distorted their aims that religious zeal became the tool of dynastic survival and aggrandizement. France was also a Catholic land, but Francis I, burning with resentment over his rejection as Emperor and recklessly determined to diminish Habsburg power, declared war in the very week when the new and catastrophic future was shaping itself at Worms. England was still a Catholic country, but Henry VIII, slippery as always, was half-heartedly supporting France – although the grand alliance which Francis had tried to organize at the Field of the Cloth of Gold the year before had come to nothing. In 1525 the Imperial troops defeated Francis at Pavia and had him brought as a prisoner to Madrid. For eight months the French king languished in prison, holding out against the ransom terms and earning for Charles a reputation for unforgiving ruthlessness. Finally he agreed to restore what France still held of Burgundy, including Dijon itself with the tombs of the great dukes, to join Charles against the Turks, and to take Charles's sister Eleanor as his bride. But he had no intention of keeping his promises. Already, in prison, he had been secretly negotiating with the Turkish Sultan. Once home he quickly organized a remarkable alliance, or 'League', to continue the fight against the would-be unifier of Christendom. It consisted of England, Milan, Venice, Switzerland, all supported by the new Pope, Clement VII, Leo's cousin – all this at a time when Europe, most particularly Venice, to say nothing of the Habsburg Austrian lands and the Christian kingdom of Hungary, were directly and increasingly threatened by the Turks, who were already in full occupation of the capitals of the Christian Serbs and Croats.

The League soon disintegrated. The Imperial army in Italy, which had defeated Francis, now hungry, unpaid, desperate, turned on their commanding general and marched on Rome, a wild, undisciplined mob, bent on loot and rapine, and led now by, of all people, the Constable of Bourbon, who had deserted his Valois king in his moment of defeat and joined the Imperial, the Habsburg, cause. Ironically, too, the Imperial army contained many German followers of Luther who saw the Pope as anti-Christ. In May 1527 they reached Rome. The Bourbon, shining in his white cloak, was struck down by an arquebus bolt in the first assault on the walls (Benvenuto Cellini was later to boast that he himself had loosed the bolt), and there was nobody to control the murderous rabble of an army which now took the city by storm, looting, burning, raping, murdering for ten days on end, running the Pope and the cardinals to earth in their refuge in the castle of St. Angelo.

Charles had no part in this. He was far away in Madrid. But it was he and nobody else who held Francis prisoner for seven months. He was master now. He held all Italy, as no Emperor had held it since the last great Hohenstaufen. The Pope existed by his favour, and early in 1530 that same Pope crowned him in a blaze of splendour at Bologna (Rome was in ruins, sacked, swept by plague, a graveyard). France was cast down. Charles, just thirty years old, master of Spain, of Italy, of the riches of all the Burgundies, of the Austrian lands, his *conquistadores* striking deep into the treasure of the Americas, Emperor of the German lands, might have seemed to have achieved an unsurpassable pinnacle of glory. It was an illusion. In the year before the humiliation of the Pope, England had broken away from Catholic Europe. France, though cast down, was still a formidable power. Lutheranism was running through Germany like a forest fire – and Charles had neither the desire nor the means to conduct a civil war in Germany. On top of everything else the Turks were still threatening Vienna.

The first great Turkish breakthrough was at the battle of Mohacs in the Hungarian plain when Suleiman's hordes advancing up the Danube towards Buda found themselves faced by Louis, King of Hungary and Bohemia, the head of an army of twenty-five thousand. There were nearly half a million in the Sultan's forces, moving with ease over the dry, flat plain under a broiling August sun. They swept across that empty landscape as far as the eye could see, and in depth they came on like a cloud of locusts armed with steel and thundering fire from innumerable cannon, their wheels chained together. Hardly a Hungarian survived that terrible day. Most lay dead on the battlefield. Two thousand, taken prisoner, were slaughtered on the following day. Louis himself was killed. It was the end of Hungary as an independent kingdom; it was also the prelude to Habsburg dominion.

Straight from the Diet at Worms, Charles's young brother Ferdinand had ridden off to take up residence in Innsbruck and preside over the hereditary Austrian lands, and Charles also, to fulfil his grandfather Maximilian's great design, married Anna of Hungary. At the same time Anna's brother, Louis, had married Ferdinand's and Charles's sister, Mary, also as promised by Maximilian. The agreement then had been that if Louis died without heirs, Ferdinand, his brother-in-law, should take the crowns of Hungary and Bohemia. The occasion had now come.

The Bohemian crown was electoral, but Ferdinand's 'election' was very quickly arranged. The Hungarians put up more resistance. The old pretender to the Hungarian crown, Janos Zapolya, still had his own army which he had not committed at Mohacs. With French support he got himself elected king. But Ferdinand, with the authority of the Imperial Diet behind him, marched on Buda and turned him out. All this took place during a lull in the Turkish onslaught. The Turks in Central Europe, like the Tatars in Russia, were raiders on a monumental scale. They would advance in a series of great waves and then, with the onset of winter, fold up their golden tents and retire. By the time of Mohacs they had quite absorbed Serbia and eastern Hungary, but they did not stay. Three years later, in May 1529, they swept back to Buda and beyond, right up to the walls of Vienna, this time with Zapolya and his army in their ranks. While the main army sat down to besiege Vienna, the outriders ranged far up the valleys of the Danube and the Enns, reaching as far as Regensburg and spreading destruction where they rode. For three weeks sixteen thousand under Count Nicholas Salm held the city against an investing army of two hundred and fifty thousand. But it was an early winter. It began to snow on 17 October, and the tented host raised the siege and moved back deep into Hungary and beyond. Three years later, in 1532, the same thing happened all over again. But this time Ferdinand was not alone. Charles, at the summit of his power, got together an imposing international army to go to the rescue of his brother, and the Turkish horde once more receded, leaving only a host of irregular horsemen to harry and burn where they could. It was after this that Ferdinand came to the uneasy arrangement with the Sultan for which he has always been blamed. He undertook to buy a modified truce for an annual tribute of thirty thousand ducats. It is hard to see what else he could have done. He was King of Hungary, but more than half Hungary was under Turkish occupation and large numbers of the Hungarian nobility and gentry found it advantageous to accept Moslem rule. The rest abandoned their estates and their ancient capital

51

and moved into the western extremity of their land, setting up their Diet in Pressburg across the river from Vienna and only sixty miles downstream.

Thus was born the new Central-European Empire of the Habsburgs, and Ferdinand, Archduke of Austria, King of Hungary, King of Bohemia, and later, after his brother's abdication, Emperor, was thus the father of a great new power.

Vienna, then, was very much a border fortress city, pent up within narrow walls. Graz in Styria, Innsbruck in the Tyrol, Prague in Bohemia, were all more comfortable places to live in. The Turkish menace was to persist, ever present, for a century and a half to come. It was not until 1683, when the immense and terrible army of the Grand Vizier, Kara Mustapha, was overcome and totally destroyed outside the city walls, that the Viennese could at last breathe freely and stretch their limbs, breaking out into the brilliant, long-delayed flowering which was to express itself in the marvellous and flamboyant building of the high baroque. By that time Spain had been long diminished as a power and a few years later the Habsburgs lost it for ever.

In the years after the sack of Rome, at Charles's court in Madrid, it was still possible to imagine that a new European order was being forged. Charles himself, aloof, unostentatious and dry by temperament, married since 1526 to Isabella of Portugal, whom he deeply loved, his only known vice an inordinate passion for rich and extravagant eating, was aware of the value of show. Even when weary, he faithfully presented himself as the glittering centrepiece of the tournaments, pageants, processions and parades which were a feature of the age. His court was cosmopolitan to a degree. The nobility of Burgundy, Italy and all the Germanies, other lands too, sent their sons to be his courtiers. The ancient Burgundian Order of the Golden Fleece became an international badge of Imperial exclusiveness. Outside Spain the family was everywhere. Margaret, the beloved aunt, still held the Netherlands firm for the Emperor. His sisters were now queens of France, Portugal, Hungary and Bohemia, Denmark, Norway and Sweden. Catherine of Aragon, his maternal aunt, was still married to the English king. His brother Ferdinand in Vienna, in Graz, in

Innsbruck, still worked in perfect harmony with him. In 1527 Isabella blessed him with a son and heir.

But France was still the enemy and a formidable power. And Germany itself was breaking up along religious lines.

In 1526, the year before the sack of Rome, an Imperial Diet was held at Speyer in Bavaria. With the papal party weakened hopelessly by the conflict between the Pope and the Emperor, who was not present, the Lutherans had things very much their own way. The Edict of Worms, which had put the Imperial ban on Luther, was annulled and it was agreed that all the numerous German states should have the right to decide on their own forms of religion. By then Luther had become a very great figure indeed. He was favoured by many of the German princes not only because of his defiance of an Italian Pope and a too powerful Emperor, not only because his dramatization of a more personal form of religion had a strong appeal to thoughtful men, particularly in the North, but also because, though a rebel of conscience, his authoritarian nature made him a fit companion and adviser of princes who did not aspire to absolute dominion. He had come to depend on such men, moreover, having alienated the lower orders, who might have flocked to him, by urging extreme measures of repression on the princes in their resistance to the dangerous peasant revolt which developed into the ruinous Peasants' War of 1524–5. Further, having moved rapidly from the nobility of his solitary resistance to papal and Imperial power at the Diet of Worms into a leader of men, he had also moved from his attempt to reform the Catholic Church into organizing an opposition church of his own. He needed the help of secular authority to bring unity and order to the ranks of his own followers. He was in the process, that is to say, of founding an institutionalized religion which would work hand in hand with those princes who would give it their protection. After the first Diet of Speyer he could go to work openly.

Three years later, in 1529, as Charles approached the apotheosis of his coronation at the hands of a defeated Pope, the Emperor decided to make a supreme effort to settle this religious schism before it got finally out of hand. He convened a second Diet at Speyer. This time the Roman party was in the majority. The agreement to allow each German state to prescribe its own religious form was rescinded. It was too late even to attempt to put a ban on Lutheranism, but those parts of Germany which had accepted it were required to give protection to the Catholics in their midst and to endow their churches, monasteries and schools. On the other hand, in the Catholic states Lutheranism was formally proscribed.

Luther and his supporters, a minority, entered a formal protest, It was a protest not against Roman doctrine. It was a protest which was not bound up with doctrine as such. It was a protest against the reversal of the decisions of one Diet by a later one, an affair of Imperial politics. Above all, it was a protest against coercion of a minority by a majority in matters of religious conscience. Protestantism had been born.

Charles still refused to give up. He knew he was facing now not merely the challenge of a single heretic but a widespread movement of protest against authority already expressed in the emergence of sects, some of them turning to violence, all struggling among themselves. On the highest level of consciousness the splendid Zwingli in Berne had already broken with Luther over the concept of the Eucharist, which he insisted was 'just a meal like any other'. He was to die a year later, but the young Calvin, in Paris, was preparing to take up his torch. The Anabaptists had survived the execution of their leader, Müntzer, and the defeat of the Peasants' Revolt. Under John of Leyden they were soon to seize the city of Münster and keep it for two years, setting up the Kingdom of New Zion practising polygamy and holding all property in common. This very fragmentation of a reform movement which, under its first leader, was responsible, orderly, and ready to work with secular authority, led both the Lutheran princes and Charles to press urgently for the calling of a grand council of all Christians to hammer out an agreed body of doctrine and authorize very necessary reforms. But not even Charles could persuade the Pope he had once held prisoner to act. The opportunity was allowed to pass, and the years went by punctuated by a long series of abortive conferences with Catholics and Protestants moving ever farther apart. Charles, with his determined efforts to induce them to compose their differences, was pitting himself against the spirit of the times. Pope Clement VII died in 1534. When, at last, his successor, Paul III, made his supreme effort and convened the Council of Trent in 1545 it came fifteen years too late.

The Council of Trent was to meet intermittently for eighteen years. It was transferred from Trent to Bologna because of the plague. It was punctuated by the efforts first of Charles, then of his brother and successor as Emperor, Ferdinand I, to reach some sort of compromise. But neither Catholics nor Protestants were in a mood for compromise. Instead of being a general council of Christendom, it developed into the instrument whereby the doctrines and the institutions of the Catholic Church were formalized for centuries to come. Even as the Council was sitting, the Protestant princes of Germany, together with Switzerland and Denmark, came together under Frederick of Saxony to form the League of Schmalkalden in resistance to Imperial pressure. Faced now with a formal military alliance, Charles had either to reconcile himself to seeing Germany split in two or to crush the League. In 1546 he declared war, and on 24 April 1547, won what appeared to be a decisive victory at Mühlberg – largely owing to the brilliant generalship of Duke Maurice of Saxony who, though a Protestant himself, supported Charles for reasons of ambition – and was rewarded with the Electorship of Saxony. The League was broken and Charles was triumphant. But not for long. The forces of the Reformation were too strong to be broken by a single battle. Further, they were harnessed now to dynastic ambition. Suddenly, while Charles was at Innsbruck, he heard that Maurice had turned his coat, had remembered that he was a Protestant, and at the same time had engineered an unholy alliance with the Catholic French. Before he could even gather an army the Emperor, ill, in excruciating pain, had to flee across the Brenner Pass where the snow still lay deep. By the Treaty of Passau in 1552, signed by Maurice and Charles's brother Ferdinand, the way was clear for the Diet of Augsburg in 1555, which gave to every German prince and every city state the right to choose its own form of religion. In the following year, his dream of a lifetime in ruins, worn out at fifty-six, racked by pain, white-haired, Charles made his farewell in the great hall of the dukes of Brabant at Brussels. He had already made over the kingdom of

Naples to his son Philip, whom he had married to Mary Tudor of England. Now, surrounded by all the panoply of his nobility and his knights, he set in train the long and elaborate process of surrendering everything he had. It was in the very hall where he had first knelt to dedicate himself as a boy of fifteen. 'If I give way to tears, gentlemen, do not believe it is on account of the sovereignty of which I am stripping myself at this moment. It is because I must leave the country of my birth and say farewell to such lieges as I have here.' For thirty-five years he had fought and striven for the dream of one Europe, one world. He left two worlds angrily embattled against each other.

He had one more journey to make, to the monastery of San Geronimo de Yuste in the heart of Spain. He had two more years to live. There was nothing ascetic about those years. He lived in perfect luxury, ministered to by a miniature court of fifty, continuing to defy his gout by eating rich and rare foodstuffs brought to him on mule-back packed in ice and nettles: oysters and fish from the Atlantic coast, pâté, game and pies from the Netherlands. He was surrounded by his books, by precious objects, tapestries and pictures, pottering with his fantastic collection of clocks. He lived like a king, but a king without responsibility, without care, more comfortably than ever before in his life, while the divided world went on outside.

After the Battle of Mühlberg in 1547, Titian had come to Augsburg to paint him in full armour, mounted, his lance on his arm, against a dark and livid sky. It was a moment of triumph for Charles; but this painting, one of the most extraordinary masterpieces of Western art, was prophetic. The horse and the armour were black, the figure of the Emperor grizzled and defiant, looming against wild clouds, a figure of a dauntless warrior, but also of a man who was lost, victorious in battle but defeated by invisible forces which he could not comprehend.

4

The Spanish apotheosis:
Philip II and the Austrian cousins

CHARLES left not only a deeply divided Europe; he left also a
divided family inheritance. His brother, Ferdinand, was Emperor.
But Philip, his son, was King of Spain. He was King of Naples and
Sicily too, Duke of Milan, lord of the Franche Comté and all the
riches of the Netherlands. He was the ruler of the Barbary Coast,
of Tunis, of the Canaries, of the Cape Verde Islands, the Phil-
ippines and the Spice Islands. He was master of Mexico and Peru,
much of the West Indies and large parts of the North American
continent. He was immensely richer and immensely grander than
his uncle the Emperor, and Charles had intended that he should
be Emperor when Ferdinand died.

This had been the cause of the only quarrel between the two
brothers, and it had been a most bitter quarrel, conducted for the
most part in a face-to-face confrontation at Augsburg which
dragged on through the latter part of 1551 and the early months
of 1552. Ferdinand, who had never made any demands on Charles,
surprised and angered his brother by insisting that his son, Maximilian, should inherit the Imperial crown. Charles was adamant:
after Ferdinand his own son, Philip, must be Emperor. There
was reason in this. Increasingly with advancing age Charles was
driven by the fragmentation of Germany to see Spain as the real
power base of the Habsburgs. He himself had no national attach-
ments: he was supranational. But the new reality lay in national
power. Spain and the Netherlands between them pressed in on
France. To strengthen the Netherlands he needed an alliance
with the English, who still held Calais and who also looked
to the Netherlands as a bastion against France. Hence Charles's

satisfaction when he married Philip off to the English queen, Mary Tudor, in 1554.

Charles expressed for all to see his new consciousness of the importance of Spain when he decided to return there to end his days. Philip took it quite for granted. By birth and upbringing Philip was in fact a Spaniard and the haughty reserve of the Spanish grandee reflected his own nature. He had not been a prepossessing youth. His cousin, Maximilian of Austria, won all hearts: he had something of the outward-going gaiety, charm and generosity, the eager curiosity, too, of his magnificent great-grandfather, Maximilian I. Almost certainly the determination of Charles to make Philip Emperor one day was fortified by his irritation and distress at the knowledge that Maximilian was preferred to his son by all the world except the Spanish world. For Philip was withdrawn, a little sickly, cutting no sort of figure at all, disliked by everyone who met him and not seeming to care whether he was liked or not. Nevertheless, in the Titian portraits of him as a young man, there is clearly visible an intensity, a suggestion of implacability, directed also against himself, which foreshadows his future growth. There is no doubt that Philip's pulse beat slowly. There is equally no doubt that he had steeled himself not to care. His coldness was in part the consequence of obsessive self-discipline, which became a habit. His letters to beloved members of his own family show a spontaneity and warmth, a tenderness and a lightness of touch the very antithesis of the outward image. His personal life, however, was nobody's business but his own. He was Philip II, King of Spain. His task, self-appointed, was to transform his realm into an absolute monarchy. His dominions included many peoples but, unlike his father, he took no pride in their variety. His far-flung lands were seen as tributary to Spain, and the business of Spain was centred in his person. He was the most devout of Catholics. He strove and fought all his life to extend the Catholic faith. But it was he who was the upholder of the faith, and Rome itself must bow to him as King of Spain, the supreme Christian monarch. He would not take a step without the approval of his spiritual advisers; but he made sure that those advisers agreed with what he was doing: he argued hard and long, and they had no choice but to approve.

Every other monarch of the day committed arbitrary and treacherous acts of violence. It was left to Philip to exalt into a philosophy the principle of the end justifying the means. He knew exactly what he was doing. When, for example, in 1570, he ordered the murder of Baron de Montigny, the envoy of Egmont and Horn in the Netherlands, and had it given out that the murder was a natural death, he did not try to pretend to himself or his trusted subordinates that it was an unfortunate accident. When he felt compelled to seize and incarcerate his unhappy and half-imbecile heir, Don Carlos, he made no bones about it. It was given out that Don Carlos had died in prison 'of his own excesses'. He may well have done. Equally well, Philip may have ordered the murder of his son. He was perfectly capable of such an act. He was also perfectly capable of confessing publicly to it. If he did cause Don Carlos to be killed, his only reason for not announcing the fact would be a careful and considered conviction that it would be too much to expect common humanity to understand why kings must sometimes kill members of their own families. How unlike his formidable contemporary, Ivan the Terrible of Russia, and his successors through the ages. How different, if it comes to that, from Henry VIII of England. . . .

Philip did not enjoy murder; he was not in the least a sadist. He murdered if, after long and deliberate cogitation, reasons of state appeared to him, rightly or wrongly, to urge the necessity for killing. He did not enjoy being present at an *auto-da-fé* in his Spanish homeland any more than he enjoyed letting the Duke of Alva loose to commit atrocities against the rebellious Dutch. It was simply that on occasion it was in the best interests of the state to burn and disembowel. There were also occasions, he considered, when those interests could best be served by a display of mildness. Thus, for example, he sought actively to restrain the zeal of his English wife, Mary, for burning heretics at the stake. He was the State no less than the Bourbon Louis XIV. But he served God devotedly according to his lights and would have endorsed slow torture rather than live a day unshriven.

So this pale-faced, shortish, slight, slowly pacing potentate, dressed invariably in black relieved only by the small, discreet white ruff, the white lace cuffs, his only ornament the Golden

Fleece hung not from its decorative chain but, like an eyeglass, from a thin black cord, has come down to us as a cold, inhuman, terrible figure, unfeeling, unseeing, remote from all common understanding, at the same time lethargic, cautious to the point of timidity, afraid to have near him any man of outstanding ability – the implacable countenance of Catholic bigotry in a bigoted age.

It is an inadequate image. Philip was the first truly professional national monarch. His task was to consolidate his realm and hold its scattered parts together to the greater glory of Spain, himself, and God. Everything was calculated to this end, and achieved with supreme economy of effort, like the working of a perfectly designed machine. He spoke always in a tone a little above a whisper: all the better to make people listen. He could freeze with the slightest of smiles, 'a smile which cut like a knife'; it saved him the necessity of frowning. He kept his most powerful grandees very much at arm's length; but he was not in the least afraid of them – he feared only God – he simply did not trust them, and with reason; they would reduce his power if they could. He alone was responsible, to God; with his confessors at his elbow he centralized all the affairs of his realm on himself, working through lesser men whom he treated and trained as civil servants.

He was, indeed, the most capable man in his realm, if only because his scheming and far-sighted and extremely subtle mind went with quite extraordinary courage. His impassivity was never broken. When he met with disaster he did not even shrug it off: he stared it for a moment in the face, measured it exactly, and proceeded to pick up the pieces and build anew. Thus when, in 1588, his great Armada which was to have delivered his crushing blow, long planned, to England, was utterly destroyed, he did not repine. 'I sent my ships against men,' he observed, 'not against the waves. Thank God that I can place another fleet upon the sea.' And this he proceeded to do. With all this he had a heart. Mary of England he did not care for at all, though she loved him. But when, after Mary's death, he failed in his efforts to persuade the new queen, Elizabeth, to marry him, and turned from England to France and married Elisabeth of Valois, he loved her tenderly and dearly. He is pictured always as wholly sedentary and retiring, immured in his private apartments in the vast and lowering Escorial, weaving his schemes, conducting his business from his table, never stirring. In fact he moved about a good deal, appearing everywhere in his short black cloak, the familiar black cap, like a brimless billycock, covering his premature baldness. And although the central, brooding sombreness of his long reign was at odds with the panache and glitter and grandeur of his treasure fleets and the gold and silver and exotic splendours pouring across from the Americas, he had in fact started off in a blaze of personal glory when, with the Spanish-hating Pope Paul IV in league with the French against him, he astonished Europe with the power and brilliance of his arms at the battle of St. Quentin (1557). His English ally, his queen, lost Calais, and thus her last foothold on the continent of Europe, but Philip had the Pope and Henry II of France at his feet. Unlike his far more attractive and free-ranging father, he was not in the least vindictive, and as a good Catholic he considered it unfitting to press home his advantage over the Pope. He had established himself, nevertheless, not merely as the great inheritor but as a formidable figure in his own right.

As such he was to preside over a great part of Spain's 'golden century' and, at the same time, to sow the seeds of its decline. His tragedy, born of his great gifts as a professional ruler and his overweening self-confidence, was his failure to perceive that he was constructing a system of absolutist government which was bound to shackle his people, impede the free development of talent and of feeling, and prove wholly pernicious in the hands of a lesser man. At the same time he had no understanding of constructive economics and fastened on his country a taxation system which proved ruinous. The treasure streaming in from the Americas gave an illusion of unlimited wealth; the brilliance of Spain's generals and the superb training of the Spanish infantry gave the illusion of invincibility. In fact the economic system ensured that, with all her imported riches, Spain was invariably hard up. And, as time went on, the devastating raids of the British seamen began seriously to affect the flow of treasure.

Indeed, in the beginning, the wealth of the Netherlands had meant more to Spain than all the treasure of the New World. By

1566, resentful of the reduction of their powers, goaded by the introduction of the Inquisition from Spain, the rich nobles of the north raised their people in full revolt. Philip's first instinct was to conciliate. Then, taking advice from his new viceroy, the Duke of Alva, he decided on a policy of repression. It did not work. Tackling the task of subjugation with unsurpassed ruthlessness, Alva did not succeed in subduing the revolt. He succeeded only in destroying the commerce on which Spain had depended for so long. Soon England, France, even cousinly Austria, all properly jealous of Philip's power, were variously exploiting the continuing revolt to their own advantage. Not even the glory of the crushing defeat of the Turks in the great sea battle of Lepanto (the Spaniards led by Charles's bastard son, Don John of Austria) could take away the taste of the continuing *débâcle* in the north. And now Philip, for the first time, lost his balance. The Netherlands had to be held and subdued. They might be held but they could not be subdued so long as other powers lent them their support. The root of the evil was the refusal of Europe to recognize the untouchability of Spain. Europe must therefore be taught. There must be a new European order, not under the Imperial crown (the Habsburg Austrian line was firmly holding on to that: it was now essentially a Germanic crown), but under Spain and its great monarch.

Now began the period for which Philip is remembered. Once he had made up his mind no holds were barred. In every country in Europe he set about stirring up trouble and intrigue on a scale, with a ruthlessness, with a conscious duplicity, never to be approached again until the advent of the Russian Communists. At the same time, in 1580, he struck. First he overran Portugal and took the crown for himself. Then he engineered the assassination of William of Orange. Then, joining forces with the Guise faction in France, burning with resentment at the favouring of the Huguenots by the French king, Henry III, he succeeded in plunging France into a disastrous civil war. That was in 1585. Meanwhile his lieutenant, Alexander Farnese, the able and powerful son of his own half-sister, Margaret, his father's bastard daughter, had been making such good progress in the Netherlands that England sprang to arms, sent troops to the Netherlands and encouraged and organized the activities of the privateers in the West Indies and the Spanish Main. In 1588, after the humiliation of the Spanish fleet in Cadiz by Drake, the crushing blow was delivered. The great Armada sailed, not to fight a sea-battle, but to convey for the invasion of England a host of Spanish infantry which would be augmented on the way by troops from Holland.

The disaster which befell this immense sea-borne expedition would have broken a lesser man. Philip quietly and patiently set himself to build up another great fleet to transport another great army. He was already sixty-one, but he behaved and planned as though he would live for ever. In fact he had another ten years, but the opportunity to subdue Elizabethan England had gone. He was now quite taken up with France. The murder of Henry III laid France wide open to Spanish domination. Only the will and courage of Henry of Navarre stood between Philip and what was now his supreme goal. It was at this moment of crisis that Alexander Farnese, Duke of Parma, the only man in Spain who could have outfought Henry, died. In the following year, in 1593, Henry adjured the Huguenot faith ('Paris is worth a mass'), received absolution from the Pope, and could now unite all the main parties in France behind him.

There were no more bastards of Charles V, or children of his bastards, to save the Netherlands. It had been a remarkable succession. Margaret of Austria had ruled successfully for eight years. Then, after the savage failures of Alva and Requesens, Don John of Austria had held the situation, and Margaret's son, Alexander, had improved it. With the death of Alexander all was falling into ruin. In 1597 Spain was formally bankrupt and Philip repudiated his debts. In 1598 he died, after an appropriate spell in purgatory, still in his little black cloak, his black cap, his Golden Fleece, to join the heavenly throng before which he kneels in El Greco's celebrated 'Dream of Philip II of Spain'. No man had worked harder for his faith. No man had served it more disastrously. All the same, he was remembered warmly in the thoughts of the plebeian John of the Cross and the nobly born Theresa of Avila, whom he defended stoutly from the wrath of ecclesiastical authority.

Habsburgs were to rule in Spain for just over a century after Philip's death, but the virtue had gone out of them. His successors ruled with all the apparatus of absolute monarchy, but both Philip III and Philip IV gave their power entirely into the hands of the sort of people the great Philip had so coolly and resolutely kept down. Philip III's reign was distinguished by the expulsion of all the Moors which wrecked the economy. Philip IV (1605–65) took a lively interest in the marvellous flowering of the arts which coincided with his reign. Velazquez was in fact his court painter and as such executed the magical series of portraits of Philip's daughter, the Infanta Margarita Teresa, destined for the marriage bed of the future Leopold I of Austria. But both these Philips were wholly ruled by others: the first by the Duke of Lerma, the second by the Count of Olivares. Lerma continued the struggle with the Netherlands; Olivares lost Portugal and Roussillon and brought Spain to the point at which she had to recognize the independence of the United Provinces, now Holland. Finally, in 1665, Philip IV was succeeded by his half-imbecile son, Charles II. He was the last Habsburg to rule in Spain. He had no children. For over thirty years the only point of interest in his life was the likely date of his death. When, very belatedly, he did die, Europe went up in flames as Habsburg, wholly Austrian now, fought Bourbon for the crown of Spain, and lost it.

The remarkable thing is that during all this time, from the death of Philip II in 1598 to the death of Charles II in 1700, Spain was regarded throughout Europe as a power of the first importance, such was the magic of the real power and personalities of Charles V and his son, and the brilliantly deserved reputation of Spanish arms developed by Philip II and inherited by his immediate successor. As time went on the Austrian branch of the Habsburgs grew in significance and strength. But no eyes looked at Austria; all eyes looked at Spain, while gradually, imperceptibly, the Central European Empire was consolidating itself and developing into one of the great powers of the modern age, even as Spain decayed.

There was plenty of excuse for this. The Austrian Habsburgs held the Imperial Crown, but they themselves looked jealously and suspiciously to Spain as the senior branch. Immense pains were taken to strengthen the bonds between Vienna and Madrid by marriage. Ferdinand and his son Maximilian sent their own children to the Spanish Court to be educated in the ways of kingship. There was, moreover, a notable lack of apparent conviction in the manner in which from 1576 the Austrian Habsburgs managed their affairs. Maximilian I, Charles V, Philip II had provided a remarkable succession of outstandingly able monarchs, and the blood had also run strongly in Charles's bastards, Don John of Austria and Margaret of Austria and her own son, Alexander Farnese. Ferdinand I had held his own and had ably seconded his brother Charles, turning Vienna into a presentable capital and diffusing his own deep cultural interests, above all his passion for music. But when he died in 1564 he hesitated to make over his whole realm to his first-born. Maximilian had Austria, Bohemia and Hungary; but one younger brother, Ferdinand, was given the Tyrol, another, Charles, received Styria, Carinthia, Carniola and Gorizia.

This was partly reinsurance. Ferdinand had had trouble with Maximilian. At first he was wild, then he moved into a state of sulky rebellion against his uncle, Charles V, for excluding him from the Imperial succession and his father for giving way. Worse, with all his notorious dissipation, he had a lively and enquiring mind, and that mind, stimulated by his general mood of revolt, was carrying him rapidly towards Lutheranism. Indeed, he went very far. Ferdinand was in no way a fanatic and was perfectly ready to tolerate Protestantism in his German lands. But with Charles dead and unable any more to insist on the Imperial crown for Philip, the German princes had made it plain that they would not have a Spaniard for their Emperor. Maximilian was his obvious choice, but his father had formally to warn him that if he flirted with Protestantism the crown could go to his younger brother. In 1562 Maximilian solemnly swore to live and die a Catholic. In 1562 he was elected King of the Romans at Frankfurt. In 1564 Ferdinand died and Maximilian was Emperor.

He was a very good Emperor, once he had settled down. He kept his word about remaining faithful to the Catholic religion, but this only made things easier for his Protestant friends. To the despair of his Spanish wife Maria, his first cousin from Madrid, a dull girl whom he had married most reluctantly in his rebellious years, he maintained the best of relations with his Protestant subjects all his life and in the end he died in 1576, fully conscious, successfully fighting off the last sacrament. His wife, his sister from Bavaria, his son Matthias, the papal legate and the Spanish ambassador, all gathered by his bedside at Regensburg to wrestle for his soul. In vain. No, he would not see a priest: 'My priest is in heaven', he declared.

He meant this. Wild as he had been, and given to high living, he believed in God and he believed in freedom of conscience. To an affronted papal legate he once declared: 'I am neither Papist nor Evangelical, but Christian.' Throughout Austria, Bohemia and Hungary there was perfect toleration. Apart from a short war against the Turks, Maximilian spent all his energies in the twelve years of his reign (he died at forty-nine) in trying to compose religious differences within the Empire as his uncle had done before him – and, as far as his own hereditary lands were concerned, far more successfully. His enlightenment was real and profound, nurtured on his exchange of ideas with some of the most independent-minded Protestants of the day and sustained by a personal sensibility which, for all his stubbornness and quick-temper, abhorred violence and coercion. He was horrified when his cousin Philip incarcerated the unfortunate Don Carlos. In 1572 when he heard the news of the bloody massacre of St Bartholomew he at first refused to believe the news: his own daughter was married to the French king Charles IX who, in fact, was so overcome with a sense of guilt at allowing himself to be persuaded into the commission of this atrocity that he went into a decline. '... It is neither right nor justifiable,' Maximilian wrote to his friend, Augustus of Saxony. 'Religious matters will not be settled by the sword nor by force, but with God's word and by Christian agreement and justice.'

It was an all too brief interlude of sanity and tolerance. And even while Maximilian, ruling now from his father's unpretentious residence, the Hofburg at Vienna, gave comfort and reassurance to his subjects, he was laying up future trouble. For all his enlightenment and toleration he, too, looked to Philip's Spain as the great base of family power. There was no love lost between him and his cousin. But the family still came first, and this indestructible article of faith had a consequence in the most bizarre of Habsburg marriages. Maximilian's most beloved daughter Anne had been betrothed to Don Carlos as an act of state. At the same time two of his sons, Rudolph and Ernst, were sent to Madrid to finish their education at court, above all to make themselves known to the Spaniards against the day when one of them, surviving, might inherit Spain. For four years, from 1563, the negotiations hung fire while Philip made up his mind whether or not his son would be fit to rule. Maximilian waited with growing impatience in Vienna. Then, like a thunderclap, came the news of the imprisonment of his prospective son-in-law. Less than a year later Don Carlos was dead. It was a black time for Philip. His beloved wife, Elisabeth of Valois, was so grief-stricken by her stepson's tragedy that she fell ill and died in child-birth. Philip, impassive as ever, kept his own grief to himself. In no time at all he had decided to marry for the fourth time to achieve a new heir. Who better than Anne of Austria, his dead son's betrothed, twenty-one years old, 'all milk and roses'. The year was 1570. Philip, when he married his niece, was just forty-three and on the edge of embarking on his new career designed to make him the monarch of all Christendom. Maximilian the enlightened let it happen. He was a Habsburg too.

There was another aspect of the Spanish obsession. The two boys, Rudolph and Ernst, took all too easily to Spain, and thus the paradox ensued that the children of Maximilian the tolerant, the enlightened, brought back to the Austrian court the Spanish taint which Maximilian had so successfully erased

Maximilian himself was horrified. He too as a youth and young man had been exposed to Spanish influence and had quickly come to detest it. But it was the Spain then of his uncle Charles, who was a Burgundian first. Rudolph and Ernst were immersed in the Spain of Philip II. They were also strongly under the influence of Spanish Jesuits. When they returned to Vienna Maximilian was deeply worried by the change in them. Those humourless, proud, unbending Spanish ways made the worst possible impression on the easy-going German nobles. The great strength of the Austrian

Habsburgs had been their unpretentiousness and their ability to win the confidence of lesser princes. Maximilian told the boys 'to change their bearing'. To no effect.

The death of Maximilian at forty-nine in 1576 was a disaster for Austria and for Europe. Everything he had stood for vanished overnight, and with it the last chance of reaching a general accommodation between Catholics and Protestants throughout the Empire. The son who succeeded him, as Rudolph II, until he was compelled to surrender the crown to his younger brother, Matthias, thirty-six years later, was for all practical purposes a non-Emperor. Although, as a person, he makes a richly fascinating study, it is essentially a pathological study. His bearing on the history of the Habsburgs was wholly negative. His reign, and that of his brother Matthias, which lasted seven years, brought the Empire to a state of ruinous chaos and served as the prelude to the horror of the Thirty Years War.

Rudolph had been particularly affected by the Spanish experience. His life in the Escorial, solemn enough at the best of times, had been coloured by the tormented gloom and the sense of subterranean violence created by the long crisis of conscience on the part of the king which was finally resolved by the imprisonment and mysterious death of his prospective brother-in-law, Don Carlos, and the subsequent breakdown and death of the Spanish queen. Heaven knows what effect this brooding horror had on the mind of a sensitive, uncontrolledly imaginative youth, who had the blood of poor, mad Joanna from both his father, Joanna's grandson, and his mother, her granddaughter. On top of all this, Philip had made the boy promise to extirpate all heresy from his lands when he came into them and had him brought up by Jesuits. Ignatius Loyola had undergone his dramatic conversion in the year of Charles V's election to the Imperial crown. He had founded the Society of Jesus in 1534 and died in 1556. The capture of Rudolph by his order meant that for the first time the Jesuits, organized on military lines but accepting a discipline which was not to be matched until the Communist Party of the twentieth century, held undisputed control over the mind of the ruler of a secular state. They were to retain that control over the Austrian Habsburgs, to a greater or lesser degree, for nearly two hundred years.

Rudolph was anything but a natural ruler; but while he lacked the qualities, even the will, to rule, he clung stubbornly to the dignity of this office and made a bitter fight for it when his brothers, after thirty years, formally declared him unfit to rule. In 1593 he suffered a new Turkish invasion of Hungary and in 1604 showed himself feeble and irresolute in face of a full-scale Hungarian revolt. By that time, indeed, virtually all his dominions were seething with discontent and the Protestant princes of the Empire were so tried by his intolerance and the high-handed (but ineffective) measures he took to punish them for their faith, that they felt compelled to lay aside their own bitter dissensions. In 1608, while his brother Matthias had effectively taken over the government and brought back order to Hungary, but before Rudolph had been formally deposed as Emperor, a Protestant Union was formed under the leadership of the Elector Palatine, Frederick IV. A year later this called into being a Catholic League to oppose it, led by Duke Maximilian of Bavaria, the most individually powerful prince in Germany. For a time it looked as though the whole of Europe would go up in flames. Neither Rudolph, nor the Pope, nor the Jesuits seemed capable of understanding the massive shift in the balance of religious power which had lately transformed the face of Christendom. England had long been lost to Rome and had successfully defied the might of Spain. Philip, the great champion of the Catholic faith, was ten years dead. The Netherlands were uncontrollable. More than half Germany was Protestant. Above all, in 1598, Henry IV of France, Henry of Navarre, had brought internal harmony to France with the Edict of Nantes, which granted civil liberties and some religious freedom to the Huguenots. With Sully he restored and improved the domestic economy. He was also now the greatest soldier in Europe and had made of the French army the strongest force. Although he had changed his religion to gain the crown he set himself firmly against Roman intolerance. He promised his support to the Protestant Union of Germany and was about to march with the Protestant princes against the Catholic League when, in 1610, he was suddenly struck down by the assassin Ravaillac.

With this act the course of history was changed. Sooner or later, the way things were going on, Protestant was bound to meet Catholic in a major war. Had Henry not been killed it is inconceivable that Austria and the Catholic League would not have been utterly shattered. Catholic power would have been broken. The Habsburgs would have lost their Central European order. Spain and the two Sicilies would have been left sole champions of Rome. As it was, with the death of Henry, the Protestant Union faltered. The war between Catholic and Protestant was postponed for another decade. By that time Austria and the Empire had found a new dynamic force in the tireless and driving energy of Ferdinand II, and a new general of genius in Wallenstein, while France, under Louis XIII, managed by Richelieu, was too much caught up with its own domestic problems to afford military intervention.

For a long time before the death of Henry IV in 1610 Rudolph had been going quietly mad. It was all the sadder because, while neglecting his dominions, he had been turning Prague, where he had set up his court in preference to Vienna, into an oasis of culture and quasi-scientific enquiry. He was an eager collector and a great connoisseur – of the strange as well as the beautiful. The Breughels and the surrealist Arcimboldos now in Vienna came from Rudolph's collection, the Correggios, too. He was a patient patron of craftsmen of every kind. Above all he pursued with real passion those alchemical studies through which Western man first came to appreciate, by patient analysis, in the search for the philosophers' stone, the mysteries of chemistry and mineralogy. This bigoted Catholic was above all one of the first patrons of modern astronomy. The Dane, Tycho Brahe, moved to Prague after the death of Frederick II of Denmark, setting up the instruments of his own invention in Rudolph's garden. To Prague and Rudolph, too, came the young Kepler, to act as Brahe's assistant. Brahe was very much a man after Rudolph's heart, a man with an enquiring and penetrating mind, who was above all a practical inventor of genius. He could see by the sheer accuracy of his observations that Copernicus had erred in his explanation of the movement of the earth and the heavenly bodies, but he lacked the particular genius to arrive at the correct solution. He could invent the telescope and other instruments and record what they told him; but he could still with half his mind bow deeply to superstition. Indeed, by assuring his Imperial master that it was written in the stars that he would die by a member of his own family, he contributed to the Emperor's mental derangement. In his last years Rudolph never set foot outside the Hradčany Palace, which was vigorously guarded. In this extraordinary household on the hill above the river, the mad Emperor existed in a world of his own. Exotic birds and animals, even tigers and lions, scurried, fluttered, paced in the empty galleries and corridors. It was said that Rudolph's end was brought about by the death of two beloved eagles and a favourite lion. Against this bizarre background the genius Johann Kepler was pondering the laws governing the motions of the solar system. It is one of the ironies of history that Kepler, a Swabian, had come to Prague and the court of Rudolph, the Catholic bigot, because he had been driven from his chair at the university of Graz by Rudolph's nephew, Ferdinand, Archduke of Styria, who was later, as the Emperor Ferdinand II, to fight the religious war which Rudolph had made inevitable. It is one of the ironies of science that this unhappy, mad non-Emperor should be commemorated by a memorial that outlasts stone: by Kepler's astronomical tables, dedicated to Rudolph, long dead, in gratitude – the Rudolphine Tables, with the aid of which, man, the unstable, helpless to order or predict his own all too Rudolphine destiny, can yet glimpse the universal order and foretell the vast movements of the stars.

Poor Rudolph died childless in 1612. Matthias, his brother, also had no child. This may have been largely Rudolph's fault, because he was jealous of his brother and behaved very badly, depriving him of any sort of establishment and thwarting his desire to marry. Matthias was not an attractive character, more ambitious than able, and driven by a desire for recognition which, when at last it was fulfilled, he proved incompetent to justify. In his early days impatience with Rudolph and despair at finding a role for himself had driven him to rebel absurdly against his own House by offering himself to the Netherlands to lead them in their struggle with Spain. He discovered too late that the proud nobles of the Netherlands had no desire to be led: they wished only to use his name. He returned to Vienna to face disgrace and ignominy at the hands of his brother, whom, in the end, he was to depose by force. As

Emperor, elderly now, he was vain and frivolous, enjoying the taste of power which he had hankered after for so long. He was more tolerant than Rudolph, and made more tolerant still by his chief adviser, Cardinal Klesl, who had the intelligence to see that the Protestant movement was too strong to meet in head-on collision. The real hope for the victory of Catholicism must lie in the bitterness of dissension among the Protestants themselves. Lutherans and Calvinists abhorred each other at least as much as they detested Rome, hurled insults at each other from their pulpits, threatened violence. Besides these main branches of the antipapist movement, together with the Utraquists of Bohemia, there was a multiplication of smaller sects. Only the active threat from Rome could force them together, as in the ill-fated Union.

But Klesl was hard-pressed by more militant brothers in Christ. A new champion of the fanatics was gathering strength in Graz, the Emperor's cousin, the Archduke Ferdinand, the son of Maximilian II's younger brother, Charles. Rudolph and Matthias were childless. The dissension in the Empire was such that the Habsburgs were in very real danger of losing the Imperial succession. After long and painful consideration within the family it was decided to put forward Ferdinand as the new Emperor. And in 1618 Matthias formally abdicated as King of Bohemia and Hungary in order to make way for his nephew and place him in a strong position to carry the Imperial election when it came.

Ferdinand, already forty, had earned the reputation of being the most ruthless and fanatical Catholic of his day. In appearance he was foxy-haired, fresh-faced, bustling and affability itself. But like his uncle Rudolph, he was wholly given over to the Jesuits and often declared that had he been born into a lower estate he would himself have entered the Order. After attending the university of Ingolstadt he was called to rule over his father's Styrian inheritance, where he distinguished himself by expelling the Protestants, who made up at that time two-thirds of the population, the mathematician Kepler among them. He said again and again that he would rather live with his family in exile and beg his bread, to be spurned and insulted, to lose his life itself, than stand by and suffer injury to the true Church. He restored the old churches to the Catholics and pulled down the new churches and schools built by the Protestants. In face of the Protestant seminaries he founded Jesuit colleges at Graz and Bruck-an-der-Mur. In spite of this wholesale displacement of persons (faithful Catholic subjects were imported to take the place of the unfortunate Protestants) and the disruption of the fabric of society, he met with remarkably little organized opposition. Indeed, he showed great cleverness and foresight, quietly, over a long period, eroding the rights and privileges of the Protestants, a little at a time, until he had weakened them so radically that it was too late for them to pull themselves together and offer effective resistance.

What was even more remarkable was the passivity of the Bohemians and the Hungarians in accepting him as their new king. By a man of ruthless temper, wholly convinced that he was the instrument of God, these initial experiences must have been received as a sign that all that was needed to re-establish Habsburg rule and scatter the enemies of Rome was a touch of that firmness which had been so lacking in both his Imperial uncles. He proceeded to act on this assumption, which turned out to be quite false. The result was that fearful and destructive conflict called the Thirty Years War.

5

War and Counter-Reformation:
Ferdinand II

At the start of the Thirty Years War the Spanish Habsburgs
were still very much the senior branch of the family. By the time it
was over Spanish power had been broken for ever, and although
Philip IV of Spain was still nominally head of the family, in fact
the power had shifted from Madrid to Vienna, where it was to
remain. Thus the reign of Ferdinand II was to mark the con-
solidation of Austria, so long delayed, as the base of a major power
and the bastion of Catholicism.

Nothing could have seemed more remote in the autumn of 1618
when the Emperor Matthias, old and decrepit and anxious only to
avoid trouble, found himself embroiled by his cousin Ferdinand,
the newly proclaimed King of Bohemia and Hungary, in armed
conflict with the Bohemian rebels. Matthias had only a year to
live. Ferdinand, even before he became Emperor, had embarked
on the course which, beginning as an assertion of his kingship, was
to develop into an Imperial crusade to re-conquer the whole of
Germany for the Catholic Church and put an end to heresy. The
crusade degenerated into a general war, or series of wars, of
conquest and aggrandizement, bringing ruin and destruction,
rapine, massacre, plague and starvation to all Germany, destroying the rich commerce of the independent free cities, putting
back the development of Bohemia by two centuries, making final
and permanent the division of Germany into Protestant North and
Catholic South, at the same time establishing the ascendancy of
Catholic France over Catholic Spain. Ferdinand was defeated in
all his hopes. The last attempt to establish a unified Catholic
Empire failed. But, although he did not know it, the Austria which
Ferdinand left behind him when he died in 1637 was to stand as

74

one of the corner-stones of the European power structure for another two hundred and fifty years. It was also to come very close to establishing within its borders a multi-national state in which the benefits of the security afforded to many small and vulnerable peoples would have outweighed the injuries suffered by those peoples at the hands of a centralized autocracy.

The Bohemian revolt was sparked off by Imperial interference in Protestant affairs in contravention of the promise of toleration set out in the Emperor Rudolph's Letter of Majesty. The first explosion was the celebrated comic opera incident, the De-fenestration of Prague, when the Imperial representatives, Mar-tinic and Slavata and their secretary, were set on by a crowd of Bohemian Deputies and thrown out of a high first-floor window in the Hradčany Palace into the courtyard below. They called on the Virgin for succour as they clung to the window frame. 'Now let your Mary help you!' cried one of the rebels as they fell. A moment later, looking down and seeing that the unfortunates were still alive and limping away, he exclaimed with awed incredulity: 'By God, his Mary has helped!' The Imperial trio had landed on a rubbish-heap which broke their fall.

But the deed was done, in intention if not in fact. For once all the quarrelling interests in Bohemia, Calvinists, Utraquists, straight-forward nationalists, came together in full revolt. But could they hold together? Cardinal Klesl thought not. He advised Matthias to conciliate, and Matthias agreed. Ferdinand, who be-lieved that right was might, was angry and contemptuous. Acting with decision he had Klesl seized in the Hofburg and sent off to a fortress in the Tyrol. Coolly and with perfect courtesy, he indi-cated to his uncle the Emperor that he himself would thence-forward look after Bohemia, and Matthias gave way. The Defenestration had taken place in March 1618. It was now July. In August two separate Imperial armies moved into Bohemia to seize Prague and put the rebels down. It looked as though they had an easy task before them. On the side of the Protestant princes there was no general enthusiasm for the Bohemian cause. Only the young Elector Palatine, Frederick, married to his Stuart bride, King James's daughter, was determined to intervene. He was driven on by his ambitious, scheming, too clever by half, Chancellor Christian of Anhalt. He had dreams of glory which he was not equipped to realize. His Palatinate was in two parts, one on the Rhine athwart the Spanish line of communication between Italy and the Netherlands, the other bordering Bohemia itself, strategically placed to block the free movement of the Imperial forces. He now came forward as the champion of the rebel cause. And his first move was to enlist the services of Count Mansfeld, whose mercenary army, on the edge of disbandment and under the Imperial ban, was conveniently placed for immediate action. Battle was joined and the Imperialists were frustrated in their drive on Prague. All that winter other interested parties, above all the Elector Maximilian of Bavaria – the richest and most powerful individual of them all – and the Elector John of Saxony worked and intrigued to find a solution in the Imperial interest without war. But on 20 March, 1619, the Emperor Matthias died. The extremists in Bohemia took immediate heart, pressing all the harder because the moderates, still more all the townspeople and the peasantry who had suffered most from the autumn troubles, wanted peace. Ferdinand himself decided to put an end to things quickly, offering quite remarkable concessions if only the rebels would capitulate. It was touch and go. But the rebels could not bring themselves to trust him and they hung on. In no time at all the tide had turned. Encouraged now by the successful defiance of Imperial might at a moment when there was in fact no Emperor, Moravia and most of the Austrian provinces were moving towards open revolt. Count Thurn re-established his grip on a reluctant, unpaid Protestant army and moved on Vienna. Already it looked as though the Viennese themselves might open the gates to the investing army. But Ferdinand, whose courage and serenity in adversity has never been exceeded, held out against all demands. While cannon shots pounded the Hofburg he prostrated himself before his crucifix and then rising, turned to his confessor to reassure him and comfort him; he had been seeking counsel from the only one who could give it, had been vouchsafed it, and was now content to die in the cause of righteousness if called upon to do so. After that he received a deputation from the Austrian Estates, angry and frightened, pressing him furiously to yield to the rebel demands. He listened courteously, indulgently almost, with a maddening good humour and a total refusal even to consider giving way: the very idea was absurd. And dramatically, at that very moment, there was a clatter of hooves on the cobbles of the courtyard below. The Only True Counsellor had not been idle. Ferdinand's younger brother, Leopold of Tyrol, had sent off four hundred horsemen to the rescue, and here, in the nick of time, they were.

It was in this frame of mind that Ferdinand, at forty-two, embarked on his terrible crusade, coolly, reluctantly, ready to forgive if forgiveness were asked and if those who asked it gave themselves into his hands, but moving in a straight line with perfect and unquestioning single-mindedness, implacable towards all those, be they whom they might, who persisted in their error. He put himself forward as the champion of Christ crucified and the Holy Mother of God. But he was a crusader who assumed increasingly the attributes of God the Father. He did this at a time when the German princes were so disturbed by the prospect of fearful conflict to come that they considered choosing another to be Emperor in his place. Ferdinand was quite unmoved. With no fears at all he carried the election. He was elected only two days before Frederick, the Elector Palatine, champion of the Protestants, so fatefully accepted from the rebels the offer of Ferdinand's crown.

Frederick, amiable and presentable, obstinate but weak, and incapable of foreseeing the likely consequences of his actions, moved with his English wife from Heidelberg to Prague. A born leader, a skilled diplomat, might have been able to quell the jealousies and suspicions of the Protestant princes and engage their support, might have been able to persuade the young French king, Louis XIII, that in spite of his Catholicism he should join with the Protestants now to shatter the power of Habsburg for ever. But Frederick was neither a leader nor a diplomat. He received little or no support. And although there was a bad moment for Ferdinand when the Hungarians revolted and joined forces with the Bohemians, the Catholics rallied round the Habsburgs to put down this upstart Protestant king who had come under the Imperial ban. Bohemia, thus, was virtually alone; the Imperial forces under the veteran Bavarian general Tilly, closed in on Prague.

What followed, on 8 November, 1620, was the terrible battle on the White Hill on the outskirts of Prague, referred to ever afterwards as the Battle of the White Mountain. There Tilly destroyed the flower of the Bohemian Protestant and nationalist movement, putting an end to Czech independence for three hundred years to come. The Thirty Years War had hardly begun, but, long after it was all over, it was possible to look back and see that Habsburg Austria as a European power had been conceived amid the slaughter on that very ordinary hillside.

With Prague in his hands, with poor Frederick, the 'Winter King', a refugee (his Palatinate later to go to Maximilian of Bavaria), with the cause of Protestantism in Bohemia and Moravia quite broken while the Protestant Electors of Brandenburg and Saxony looked on, Ferdinand proceeded to assimilate the Czechs into his Austrian complex. In due course the Bohemian crown was declared a hereditary possession. Protestantism was proscribed. Immediately the survivors of the rebel leaders, twelve in number, were seized, arraigned and condemned to death. Ferdinand, whose natural temper expressed itself in slow, gradual, fairly painless but inexorable movement towards a distant but brightly shining goal (as witness his earlier and clever suppression of Protestantism in Styria and Carinthia), was not at all happy about this violence. When the list of the condemned was brought to him in the Hofburg for his signature he could not at first bring himself to sign. He stared at the document, pushed it away, paced the floor, stared at it again, got up and hurried out of the room, wiping the sweat from his forehead and leaving his advisers aghast. But he pulled himself together like a man, consulted urgently and at length with his confessors, pleaded to be shown God's will; was shown; signed. Two hundred miles away in Prague the axes fell. Twelve heads of twelve national leaders went up on spikes over the tall gothic gateway to the Charles bridge over the river Moldau

Then came the great redistribution of land. It was not planned. All the vast lands of the Protestant nobility fell to the Crown. A rich king, a rich emperor, could have held them, leasing them or bestowing them judiciously on valued supporters as rewards or as pledges for carefully stipulated support. But Ferdinand was not rich. He sold the lands, reluctantly, and at knock-down prices for what they would fetch – in a debased currency at that. The bidders came from all over Europe. The great Bohemian Catholics had the advantage, of course. Prince Liechtenstein managed to secure twenty separate estates for himself. But the new men came from everywhere. And thus arose that immensely wealthy, immensely powerful Bohemian and Moravian nobility, reigning almost like independent kings over their rich domains, and in future years all too often forgetting their obligations to the dynasty to which they owed so much, even to the point of holding, in effect, the Emperor of the day to ransom. One of the men who profited most from these forced sales was the Catholic noble Albrecht Wenzel Eusebius von Wallenstein. This furiously ambitious soldier and statesman of genius, commander-in-chief in the fighting to come and master of a virtually independent army, came under suspicion of seeking the crown for himself; falling into disgrace, he later had to be recalled as the only man who could counter the new menace from the North, Gustavus Adolphus of Sweden, who appeared like an avenging fury to shatter Ferdinand's cause at the very moment when his dream seemed on the verge of being realized.

But Wallenstein's story belongs to the history of the Thirty Years War. Ferdinand's immediate quarrel was with the Bohemians, and the fighting should have ended with the defeat of the Bohemians at the Battle of the White Mountain. The struggle, however, was kept alive by Frederick's refusal to apologize to the Emperor and ask his forgiveness. England and Spain, remarkably, agreed on a plan to restore Frederick to his own Palatinate, to send him back to Heidelberg in effect under the protection of the Spaniards who needed free passage through his territory between Italy and the Netherlands. But Frederick, stiffened in his resolution by his Scottish wife, would have nothing to do with the plan. He fled to the Hague to join forces with William of Orange, even then preparing for the Spanish onslaught which he knew must come with the end of the twelve-year truce in 1621. Frederick was going to reconquer his Palatinate himself with the aid of the Dutch. He also had a stroke of luck. The gifted soldier of fortune Count Mansfeld, who had come under the Imperial ban for supporting the Protestant cause, still had intact a well-trained mercenary army. He had nothing to lose and everything to gain by creating for himself a sort of enclave round Pilsen and building up his strength by recruiting all over Germany, and he was ready to fight for Frederick.

By 1622, Frederick was ready for a major stroke. Brandenburg and Saxony still held aloof, as they were to hold aloof for another nine years. But with Christian of Brunswick in Westphalia, with George Frederick in Baden, and with Mansfeld, who had now moved his important army into Alsace, he could now count on some 40,000 men to bring all their forces to bear on General Tilly and the Spaniards.

These allies managed to keep things going until, in 1625, England sent an expedition against the Spanish Netherlands and, much more importantly, Denmark, which already had a footing in Holstein, came freshly into the fray on the Protestant side. Tilly was now in serious trouble, but still Saxony and Brandenburg held back. And now began the sombrely glittering career of Wallenstein. He had made himself immensely rich. He was a kind of viceroy over a large part of Bohemia. He had already seen the Hungarians out of the war. Now he demanded, and received, permission from Ferdinand to raise his own army, and was victorious all the way, in conjunction with Tilly driving Denmark out of the war. Only one danger remained, the threat to the Baltic coast of Germany from Sweden, the new northern power which was preparing to strike south.

For nearly twenty years the extraordinary soldier king, Gustavus Adolphus, had been successfully fighting Denmark, Russia and Poland and had turned his army into the finest fighting force in Europe. He was now preparing to move into Germany, first bullying, cajoling, frightening Protestant Brandenburg and Saxony into at last declaring themselves for the Protestant cause, defying a Catholic Emperor against whom they had not raised a finger throughout twelve years of war. The entry of Gustavus Adolphus was largely a triumph of French diplomacy, now being conducted by Cardinal Richelieu with extreme subtlety and far-sightedness, but with the narrowest of objectives which had nothing at all to do with religion but only with the aggrandizement of France and the reduction of the Habsburg power. To this end, having settled domestic difficulties, he had invaded Italy.

Wallenstein knew all about the King of Sweden and respected him and feared him. The Spaniards, on the other hand, regarded the Swedes with Castilian disdain as obscure northern barbarians whose fifth-rate power might show to advantage in fighting over northern barbarians but was beneath the notice of Madrid. At the very moment when Wallenstein was concentrating all his strength on the coming conflict with Sweden, Philip IV in Madrid demanded the immediate despatch of Wallenstein's army to Italy: the war in Germany was over, the Spaniards thought. Furthermore, Philip's overbearing adviser, or master, Olivares, was conducting a personal vendetta against the great Spanish general, Spinola, who had ventured to disagree with him. Spinola was to be shown that his army was not needed to fight the French in Italy. Wallenstein's would do.

Ferdinand, the younger cousin, could not stand against Philip, with all the power and prestige of Spain behind him. Wallenstein, he ordered, must send 30,000 men at once to Italy – to be commanded not by him but by a Spanish general. Wallenstein flatly refused. It was his own army, and he needed every man in it to hold the Baltic coast and prevent the Swedes from landing: once they were permitted to land there would be serious trouble. In face of this flagrant disobedience to the Imperial command all the Catholic princes, who had been increasingly jealous of Wallenstein and suspicious of his intentions, came together to force Ferdinand to remove him from command. Ferdinand himself saw no other course open to him, but it was a bad moment. On the one hand he needed this great soldier, on the other he was not at all sure that Wallenstein would go quietly. What would happen if he turned on the Imperialists with all his army? Such fears were by no means exaggerated. Later Wallenstein was to show an infinite capacity for disloyalty and the most complex intrigue. But for the moment he had too much to lose: he needed to secure his own Bohemian possessions and build them up and make them economically rich and strong. He went.

The damage, however, was done. The great danger perceived

by Wallenstein at once materialized. In 1630 before Tilly, now in full command, could reach the Baltic coast, Gustavus Adolphus had landed. And now began the fantastic advance of the fighting Swedes, sweeping West and South in a great half-circle across to the Rhineland provinces, down and round to the East, deep into Bavaria and across to Austria itself. And at last, to get on the bandwaggon of the formidable King of Sweden, Brandenburg and Saxony declared themselves. If they had declared themselves sooner, Europe would have been spared one terrible episode which has been remembered as a black stain in a very dark history, and which contributed greatly to the viciousness of subsequent fighting in the Thirty Years War: the sack of Magdeburg by Tilly's troops in May 1631 and its total destruction by fire. Such savagery had not been seen in Europe since the massacres in the Albigensian War. It was to remain in memory as the symbol for supreme atrocity until the eruption of Hitler and Stalin into an age which thought Europe had finished with barbarity. It was not ordered by Tilly, who tried to stop it and was seen at the height of the violence nursing a baby snatched from the arms of its mother, dead at his feet. But it has coloured the reputation of this steady, brave, by no means brilliant fighting man; and it has coloured the memory of Ferdinand II in whose cause atrocity was done. It happened because Tilly, racing for the coast to catch Gustavus Adolphus before he could build up his strength, managed to reach Magdeburg first, and sent in his hungry and exhausted troops to reduce it in short order. Ever after, when the Swedes stormed town after town and the citizens sought safety in surrender, they would remind themselves of Tilly's massacre with the dreaded cry, 'Magdeburg quarter!', and the killing would start again.

After Magdeburg the Imperialists found themselves facing a most formidable conjunction of Sweden, the two great Protestant Electorates, the United Provinces in revolt and a hostile France actively preparing to seize the advantage where she could. Tilly was forced to run for it. In September 1631 he was utterly shattered at Breitenfeld where, for the first time, his forces, drawn up in conventional order of battle – cavalry on each wing, infantry in the centre – found themselves confused and utterly overwhelmed by the loose, checkerboard, flexible array invented by

Gustavus Adolphus – infantry in compact squares, with form-ations of cavalry disposed in the aisles between the squares, so that they could turn and move at will in any direction they chose. Seven months later, in April 1632, on the River Lech, not far from where the Emperor Otto the Great had fought his battle to save Western Europe from the Magyars seven hundred years before, much the same thing happened, and this time Tilly himself was fatally wounded.

By now Wallenstein had been brought back. In November of that same year he met Gustavus Adolphus at Lützen, and was defeated; but the Swedish king was killed. Wallenstein was now the supreme figure on the battlefield; but it was no longer the same war. Gustavus Adolphus, a warrior king possessed with the lust of conquest had at least, as a Protestant, been the figurehead of a cause. In 1632, after twenty-four years of war, the cause itself was lost. It was now a free for all. Mercenary armies fought for their own loot. German princes, Catholic and Protestant alike, fought for territorial aggrandizement. France, governed by Rich-elieu, who had two first-class generals in Turenne and the Duc d'Enghien, later to be known as the Great Condé, moved into the chaos to destroy Spanish power and make what gains she could in Germany. Wallenstein was now acting as an independent prince, intriguing with his friends and enemies alike for his own personal advantages, suspected of having designs on the crown itself. Nobody knows what this strange, reserved, bitter, equivocal, greedy, dreamer of a man (who was also a superb and enlightened ruler) would in fact have done. In 1634 he was assassinated. The effective leadership of the Imperial forces fell to the very brave and gifted young Spanish Infant who, together with Ferdinand's son, soon to be Ferdinand III, showed that Habsburgs could fight and command in battle as well as rule from palace cells.

Ferdinand II died in 1637, fighting no longer to conquer Ger-many for the true faith but to preserve his own inheritance and Spain. He did not live to see the unthinkable destruction of the invincible Spanish army by the French at Rocroi in 1643. He was spared the humiliation of the peace of 1648, which at last ended the Thirty Years War. By the Treaty of Westphalia Sweden took parts of what was later to be Prussia; Saxony held Lusatia;

Brandenburg, the nucleus of the Prussia to be, was greatly enlarged; Bavaria retained the Upper Palatinate; the Dutch Netherlands, the United Provinces, were finally torn from Spain and confirmed in their independence, to become Holland; Switzerland achieved recognition of her independence; France gained the fortress towns of Metz, Verdun and Toul, as well as nearly the whole of Alsace.

Spain, ruined by the arrogance and greed of Olivares and the feebleness of Philip IV, still held the part of the Netherlands which would one day be Belgium and vast possessions in the New World. The Spanish court was still the seat of pomp and splendour. But she would never again be a power. France now had the finest army in Europe. With the Holy Roman Empire fragmented into some three hundred independent states, with Gustavus Adolphus dead, with Prussia not yet born, with Russia barely emerged from the anarchy of the 'Time of the Troubles', with Austria finally humiliated and the principle of religious toleration formally established throughout Germany outside the Habsburg possessions, who was to challenge her? Who was to prevent her from dominating the continent of Europe, depopulated, ravaged, hoeplessly weakened by the ravages of thirty years of war? The answer was Austria, Catholic Austria, improbably allied with Protestant England. But the new pattern was to take some time to show.

6

Vienna besieged and the challenge of Louis XIV: Leopold I, Joseph I, Charles VI

FERDINAND III would have been a good Emperor in happier times. He did not inherit his father's fanaticism. He was intelligent and inclined to tolerance. He had also proved himself cool-headed and courageous in battle, as when he and his Spanish cousin had played a decisive part in the defeat of the Swedes at Nördlingen in 1634. But his whole career marked a sort of interregnum, a pause for breath and re-orientation between two great historical movements. First, for six years, between 1637 and 1643, he sought in vain for ways and means of ending a war which had lost all meaning, eager to make important concessions to the Protestants, prevented only by the determination of France and Sweden to humiliate the Imperial power. Then came the five weary years of negotiation, accompanied by continued fighting, to end in the peace of Westphalia in 1648. The nine years remaining to him were above all occupied with the slow and painful business of recovery. When he died in 1657 the outlook for Vienna was still bleak. Spain, though broken in the field, was still invested with all the accoutrements of power. Philip IV was wholly ineffective as a ruler, but he shone as a patron of the arts. It was the Spain of Velazquez and Murillo, many lesser painters too. And poets. Lope de Vega was dead, but his inspiration was still very much alive. Calderón was at the summit of his powers. There was nothing to suggest that in a very few years the substance behind the brilliance and vitality of Spanish society would crumble away. Even when it did, so firmly fixed in Vienna was the image of Spanish greatness that it took a long time for the poor Austrian cousins to realize the reversal of the roles.

Meanwhile Austria still based her dynastic policy on the multiplication of marriages between Spanish and Austrian cousins. But in 1648, the year of the peace, there was a sharp rebuff. The Emperor had married his young daughter Maria Anna to her elderly uncle, Philip IV; twice a widower, he was expecting to marry his son and heir, yet another Ferdinand, to the Spanish Infanta, Maria Teresa. But even as the bridal party made its way from Vienna to Madrid there came a peremptory message from Philip: the marriage was off. Maria Teresa had been betrothed to the child king, Louis XIV of France. The Bourbons and the Spanish Habsburgs were making it up. Vienna must look after itself.

Very soon after that the prospective bridegroom himself died of smallpox. He was twenty-one. His father, broken, died three years later. The new heir, Leopold, the second son, looked unpromising. His succession to the Imperial crown was determinedly disputed by the French, who held him in unthinking contempt, characteristically confusing his lack of surface brilliance, wit and charm with stupidity and dim-wittedness. Once again, operating now through Mazarin, Richelieu's ingenious successor, they sought with bribes, blandishments and hidden threats to secure the election of their own young king. They failed. Leopold just scraped through. The year was 1658 and the new Emperor was eighteen. Louis XIV, already embarked on the career that was to dazzle the world, was two years older. He was to regret the day that Leopold was born.

The last thing poor Leopold wanted was to rule. He was hideous and undersized, his bones stunted, his teeth broken by scurvy. He was painfully short-sighted. In him the Habsburg lip and chin were exaggerated to the point of caricature. He was pathologically shy. He would have liked to have gone into a monastery, and, indeed, from early childhood he had been intended for the Church. Instead of this he was called upon not merely to wear the crown but to carry Austria into the new course determined by the outcome of the Thirty Years War and to defend his personal Empire against the two most formidable adversaries in the world: France, arrogant and triumphant under Louis XIV, and the Ottoman Turks in their last and most terrible bid to break into

86

Europe. Out of these conflicts Vienna was reborn to become the glittering capital of legend.

Leopold's own contribution to all this was the reverse of showy. It was considerable all the same. He made fearful mistakes. He stumbled reluctantly, sometimes as a direct result of his own mismanagement, from war to war, and failed to press the advantage when he had it. He was a bigot of the narrowest kind and alienated his Hungarian subjects by harsh treatment of the Protestants and a rigid system of government. Hopelessly at a disadvantage in the handling of men, he secluded himself in his court behind a solemn barrier of protocol and etiquette taken over from Madrid, dressing always in the Spanish fashion in black with red stockings. Hidden from the world, however, he could be gay and charming. He snatched every moment he could spare for his beloved music, playing himself, composing more than well. He was happiest with his books, but he was also an alchemist of sorts and he loved painting. With the Infanta Maria Teresa betrothed to Louis of France, with his elder brother dead, a marriage was now arranged between Leopold and Philip IV's younger daughter, Margarita Teresa, his own niece. The miraculous series of Velazquez portraits of this Spanish princess at various stages of her childhood were done for Leopold as he waited in Vienna for his betrothed to grow up. This grave, blank image of immortal dreams was married at fifteen. She bore her husband five children and died in childbirth at twenty-two. Leopold was kind and gay with her. But all his life, and through two more marriages, he wrestled ceaselessly with the pangs of conscience and the necessity to make decisions, at the cost of never-ending stomach pains. He wrestled successfully, nevertheless, and he made decisions: at first he left them to his ministers until, betrayed by one of his respected grandees in his first war with the French, he took the government into his own hands and kept it there. He was to owe his survival and the rebirth of Vienna to others. But he had all the Habsburg obstinacy in defence of what was his, together with a natural shrewdness and intelligence and his share of the family capacity for a coolness in action and instantaneous recovery from catastrophe. These were the qualities that enabled him to survive his own mistakes. He held his own until first the reluctant princes of the Empire were shamed or frightened by Louis and the Sultan into rallying to his defence, and, later, under the inspiration of William of Orange (William III of England) the Grand Alliance was formed for the overthrow of France finding its instruments to hand in the genius of the Duke of Marlborough and Prince Eugene of Savoy.

Throughout all Europe the second half of the seventeenth century was dominated and conditioned by the Sun King's career of aggression and aggrandizement. Not all the splendours of Versailles can disguise the consequences of the personal rule of this extremely vulgar monarch. Indeed, they only emphasize them. He raised the world in arms against him in his lifetime and ruined a rich and splendid land for his posterity. In so far as Leopold's wars were the direct response to his challenge, it can be said that the Austrian Empire of modern times owed its very existence to the immoderation of the dynast who set out to wipe it from the map. Heaven knows Leopold asked for trouble. It was he and his advisers with their bigotry and lack of imagination who twice drove the Hungarians to rebel and invoke the armed support of Turkey. But it was the unholy plotting of a nominally Christian king, determined to set all Europe by the ears and profit by it, even to lending active support to a Moslem campaign against a Christian Emperor, which ensured that the response to Leopold's call for help from other princes threatened by the greed of France was, if not swift, at least decisive.

The first critical moment did not come until 1683, after a number of limited and indecisive wars. Then, as had happened a century and a half before under Suleiman the Magnificent, a great Turkish army swept up the Danube plain, crushing everything in its path. A quarter of a million strong, under the Grand Vizier Kara Mustafa, it reached Vienna in July and sat down to lay siege to the city.

The Turks were not nice fighters. They burned and massacred for the love of it, not in the heat of battle or victory, not in drunken rioting, but in cold blood and under precise instructions from their command. In Perchtoldsdorf, for instance, just outside Vienna, the townspeople and refugees from the surrounding countryside had taken refuge in the church and barricaded it. The Turks first burned down the little town, then sent an envoy to the church to promise safe-conduct to all inside on payment of a certain sum. The pasha in command sat himself down on a red carpet in the ruins of the village square and demanded that the keys of the church and the ransom money be brought to him by a fair-haired virgin who should carry a flag of truce and wear a crown of flowers. The village bailiff's seventeen-year-old daughter was chosen to lead the way. As the villagers emerged into the light of day they were disarmed and seized. The men were slaughtered on the spot. The pasha reserved to himself the pleasure of killing the unfortunate young girl. The rest of the women and children were sent back to Turkey to be sold as slaves. This sort of thing was happening all over Lower Austria: while the Grand Vizier's great army camped in a city of tents outside the walls, some of them silken palaces with gardens and menageries, troops of horsemen raided the countryside, burning and looting far and wide.

This was the threat, not only to Vienna but to all Europe. Kara Mustafa had vowed that he would not cease his advance until he had stabled his horses in St. Peter's in Rome. But even now the German princes hesitated to combine to meet the threat which the Christian king at Versailles, conducting his absurd rituals under the eyes of a hypnotized nobility, had striven so hard to evoke.

Leopold was not a fighting monarch. Not for him the example of his father who had risked his life at Nördlingen. It is doubtful if he was afraid of dying, but he was terribly afraid of the consequences to the Empire of his capture or his death. As the Turks approached the city he led the general flight from Vienna, lumbering in his heavy travelling coach along unmade, rutted roads up the Danube valley to Linz, then on to Passau. It was the signal for all who were fearful and could find a place in a coach or a cart to fly after their Emperor in a night of panic and confusion. But Leopold was not simply running away. He had a purpose. Summoning an Imperial Diet at Regensburg, and backed by the exhortations of the Pope, who scattered promises of indulgences far and wide, he laboured to conjure into being an imposing force under the command of a fine and steady soldier, Duke Charles of Lorraine. Many German principalities, at last recovering from the trauma of the Thirty Years War, sent their contingents to serve under Charles. At the same time the flamboyant King of Poland,

John Sobieski, was setting out from Cracow with an army of his own.

While this formidable undertaking was in progress Vienna had to stand alone. Although many had fled, the population was swollen by refugees from the country outside the city walls and the trained defenders were few. But under the command of Count Starhemberg the professional soldiers were reinforced by ordinary citizens formed and drilled into an auxiliary army; the students of Rudolph IV's old university, organized and commanded by their rector, were particularly bold and successful in making night-time forays to bring back prisoners for questioning and, more importantly, food and cattle on the hoof from the vast stores and stockyards in the Turkish camp.

All the same, after three months of incessant bombardment, the immensely thick fortifications were crumbling, and there was nothing the defenders, on the edge of starvation now, could do to hold back for much longer the patient methodical trenching and mining of an inexhaustible host of Turkish engineers. Again and again the enemy broke through the counterscarp into the dry moat below the Hofburg itself. Again and again they were driven back before they could fill the moat as a prelude to the storming and scaling of the walls. Early in September the city was shaken by an explosion more shattering than any until then. The walls at last were properly breached, and the fighting was now desperate. After four or five days of frantic and improvised defence the end seemed to have come. And then, by a miracle as it seemed, the great wooded hill, the Kahlenberg, commanding the city and the river, was seen to be alight with rockets and a myriad campfires. Sobieski and his Poles, and Charles of Lorraine with his levies from Saxony, Bohemia, Bavaria and Swabia, had at last made their junction and advanced to command the cityward slopes of the *Wienerwald* and the plain below, where Kara Mustafa lay sleeping, embowered in concubines.

The end was violent and swift. Before first light on 12 September the Imperial commanders heard mass. The Turks were now drawn up in battle array; but, with their backs to the city they had been on the edge of taking, they had to face uphill. By the afternoon they were broken, leaving all their jewelled wealth, above all their stores of food, whole stockyards, their tents, some silken, and exotic animals too; they did not draw breath until they were deep into Hungary.

This was how Austria, and much more besides, was saved by the Poles, fighting side by side for once with Germans. They did not get much thanks. Leopold was not far behind. He had been moving by boat down the Danube from Linz behind his advancing armies, and two days after the great victory he was back in the badly shattered Hofburg. Sobieski, after a thanksgiving mass and banquet in the Starhemberg Palace, had settled his troops at Schwechat, well outside the city on the level plain that led to Hungary – partly as a precaution against looting, partly to remove them from the danger of infection from the rotting corpses of men, horses, camels, which littered the fields outside the city walls. He had to be thanked, but how? It would never do for the Emperor to treat one of his generals as an equal. He fell back on protocol. The proper place to thank him was on the battlefield. So Leopold rode halfway out to Schwechat and Sobieski rode halfway to meet him. There were no embraces. When the Polish king, who had saved the throne, made his obeisance Leopold did not even touch his hat. He read out a short message of thanks in Latin, turned round, and rode back to Vienna.

Sobieski and Charles of Lorraine then got on with pursuing the Turks, shattered them again, and went on fighting for years.

Leopold took up the reins again as though nothing had happened. But there was a difference all the same. 'The little black *Herr* in red stockings' was hailed as the saviour of Europe. He faced the future with a new confidence, and that confidence, spreading through his realm, was to express itself in a sudden flowering of cultural activity, above all building in the grandest manner which, over the next fifty years, was to transform the huddled, narrow fortress city into the splendid nucleus of what, when at last the walls came down, became one of the most beautiful cities in the world. This did not happen all at once. Most of the great building was done when Leopold was dead, during the reigns of his two sons, Joseph I, who reigned only six years (1705–11), and

Charles VI (1711–40). But the clearing of the ground was done by Leopold. Most wonderfully, some of the greatest architects of the day in any country, native born, were emerging from nowhere at precisely the right moment to assimilate the baroque which numerous Italians had brought to Austria, South Germany and Bohemia for the great rebuilding of churches and monasteries after the desolation of the Thirty Years War, and to strengthen it with an infusion of gothic depth and seriousness: Bernhard Fischer von Erlach, Lukas von Hildebrandt, Jacob Prandauer and others.

This new mood was not confined to architecture, sculpture, painting. Leopold himself, though so close to the Jesuits, perceived in his cool way that his Empire needed science as well as faith. To that end this strange little man became a great founder of universities and libraries. More than this, he shocked his beloved Jesuit advisers by refusing to entrust to them the education of his children.

Behind the stiff protocol, and in spite of the extreme, slow caution of his temperament, he had indeed a tough and enquiring mind, far-ranging and well schooled. He was also practical. He carried out a systematic reform of the legal code, established a regular police force for his capital into which he also introduced street lighting – the first beginnings of public services and utilities in the Empire. Above all he responded to the needs of the times by completely reorganizing the system of military service. Gone, imperceptibly, were the days when wars were fought by small, mobile, *ad hoc* armies under virtually independent commanders and composed of mercenaries or unwilling citizens pressed into service, living wholly off the country. Towards the end of the century in the great conflict with France the armies involved might number 100,000 men properly organized into regular formations and units, supplied by their own strategically placed depots, or magazines, their movements controlled by elaborately calculated plans. When Leopold died in 1705, the year after the supreme triumph at Blenheim, he left a standing army with a regular peace-time establishment of 74,000 men which could be expanded rapidly in case of need.

The man behind this was the great Eugene of Savoy, one of the two greatest soldiers of the age and perhaps the wisest counsellor.

A tiny, frail little man with a body of whipcord, a mind like a knife, an eye like a hawk, he was one of those happy warriors who come forward at the right time and in the right place for the full deployment of their genius. The irony was that he was born a subject of the French king. He had wanted to fight for Louis, who turned him away, partly because no man ever looked less of a soldier, more particularly because of a rather lurid family history. So he offered himself to the Emperor Leopold, won his spurs under Charles of Lorraine in the destruction of the Turks under the city walls, and went on with him to play a subordinate part in the Imperial victory at Mohacs in 1687 on the very field where Suleiman had shattered the Hungarians under their King Louis in 1526. Hungary herself, exhausted, now at last submitted to the Emperor in Vienna: the Hungarian crown ceased to be elective and became hereditary to the Habsburgs.

Eugene had further triumphs ahead of him in the East. In 1697 he won a brilliant victory over the Turks at Zenta, his first truly independent command which led, by the Treaty of Karlowitz in 1699, to the cession of all Turkish-occupied Hungary to the Habsburgs. Much later, in 1717 he was to crown his career with the capture of Belgrade. But Leopold was dead by then, and much else had happened.

What above all had happened was the humbling of France, the undoing of the pretensions of Louis XIV, and the emergence of Austria as a formidable military power operating as a force in her own right and in alliances with other powers which owed little or nothing to the Imperial mystique and much to the strategic position, the material resources and the armed strength commanded by the government of Vienna.

The occasion was made by the courage and determination of William of Orange in his sustained and inspired exertions to make Holland safe from French aggression. He was by no means a brilliant soldier, but he kept the French in play and shone as diplomat and planner. When, in 1688, he accepted the offer of the crown of England and Scotland he was largely moved by the prospect of bringing England into his existing anti-French coalition with Austria. Nine years later, by the Treaty of Ryswick,

Louis was forced to sign away Lorraine, the Rhine fortresses, and all the lands he had seized since 1679, with the single exception of Strasbourg. Holland was secured in her independence and France was forced to recognize William III as King of England and to abandon her support of James II.

The next act was William's masterpiece. He knew that at any moment the last Habsburg king of Spain, the miserable Charles, would die, and this event was bound to precipitate a conflict over the succession. To be ready for the day William devoted himself to forging a Grand Alliance between the Empire (which meant Austria), England and Holland, later joined by Prussia, Denmark, Portugal and Savoy. William died in 1702, but his work was well done. When the Spanish king had at last expired in November 1700 and Louis, breaking his treaty agreement, claimed the Spanish throne for his grandson, Philip of Anjou, and installed him in Madrid, the allies were ready to fight. That is to say, they had the men and the generals; for Eugene of Savoy, fresh from his triumph at Zenta, was now joined by the Duke of Marlborough, his equal, perhaps his superior, in boldness and imagination. These two extraordinary men were to work together in miraculous harmony as no two allied commanders-in-chief had ever worked together before or have done since. It was after Marlborough had succeeded in manoeuvring the French out of one position after another that the two great commanders concerted that elaborate combined operation which was to bring them and their two armies, Marlborough sweeping down from the Netherlands, to an agreed rendezvous in Bavaria (which had entered the war on the side of the French) putting them between Vienna and the Franco-Bavarians who were marching blithely on the city. The result was the Battle of Blenheim, in the course of which both Eugene and Marlborough each had the satisfaction of coming personally to the other's rescue.

That was in 1704. In the following year Leopold died. The French Philip still sat in Madrid, but in 1703 Leopold had proclaimed his own younger son, Charles, as rightful King of Spain and sent the seventeen-year-old Archduke posting across Europe in a brilliant cavalcade of brand-new coaches painted in the Spanish colours, yellow and white, a complete court on wheels, to be set up in Barcelona.

The new Emperor was Leopold's eldest surviving son, Joseph I, who seemed the heaven-sent man to nurture and develop his inheritance at the moment of its first flowering. Fair-haired, blue-eyed and strikingly handsome under his periwig, generous, kind, physically and morally courageous, an enthusiast for the arts and sciences no less than for war, he was almost too good to be true. As Archduke he had fought in his father's army with real distinction. But as Emperor he had the sense to give his generals their heads, not interfering with their operations, and concentrating properly on the reform of his civilian government. But he had far too little time. While Marlborough and Eugene piled victory on victory, Eugene at Turin, Marlborough at Ramillies and Oudenarde, both together again in Malplaquet, Joseph in Vienna found himself victim of his father's sins. Once more the Hungarians rose up in arms against a Habsburg, their rebellion this time taking the form of a peasant war, laying waste to parts of Silesia and Moravia, penetrating the borders of Austria and bringing a formidable and dangerous people's army to the walls of Vienna itself. Joseph, who from the first had been determined to implement a policy of religious toleration and social conciliation, tried desperately to convince the Hungarians that he was, in effect, on their side. In vain. They could not bring themselves to trust a Habsburg. So they had to be fought, an operation which was carried out with a decision and sharp effect and followed, to the great surprise of the defeated Magyars, by a peace of splendid magnanimity. For the first time since the Habsburgs had held the Hungarian crown it looked as though the proud, stiff-necked and volatile Magyars could look forward to a hopeful future.

But it proved in fact too good to be true. Three months after the peace with Hungary was signed, Joseph, at thirty-three, caught the smallpox and died.

At this moment, also, the War of the Spanish Succession was drawing to its close. England under the new Tory administration was determined on peace. Already in 1710, two years after Oudenarde, Marlborough had been recalled and dismissed. Joseph's brother Charles, who had been fighting none too successfully in Spain, could still look forward, nevertheless, to the final defeat of France and to confirmation of his possession of the Spanish crown. Joseph's death upset all that. When Charles succeeded him as Emperor, the prospect of one man uniting Spain and the Empire in his person was not to be borne with equanimity. Hence what Austria was to regard as the great betrayal: by the series of treaties known collectively as the Treaty of Utrecht the Spanish crown was awarded to the Bourbon Philip V after all, on condition that no individual should ever be both King of France and King of Spain. Utrecht was finalized in 1713. Louis XIV, who had two more years to live, had salvaged that much from his humiliating war; but the Spanish Netherlands, Naples, Milan and Sardinia were taken from Spain and given to Austria. England gained Gibraltar and Minorca from Spain and kept Nova Scotia, Newfoundland, the Hudson Bay territories, as well as St Kitts in the West Indies, won from the French. She also acquired the immensely valuable monopoly of the slave trade with Spanish America, the Asiento. There were two other features of interest in the Treaty of Utrecht which were to have a radical effect on the history of Europe. The Duke of Savoy was given Sicily (which he afterwards exchanged with Austria for Sardinia) and promised a kingship: in due course all Italy would be united under the Sardinian crown. Most important still, the powers formally confirmed the elevation of the Elector of Brandenburg as King of Prussia: Leopold, as Emperor, had made him king in return for his adherence to the Grand Alliance.

Spain or no Spain, Austria was great; but she no longer had a great ruler. Joseph, had he lived, would almost certainly have succeeded in pulling his sprawling and scattered inheritance together, providing reasonable government in the Netherlands and Italy, centralizing the Austrian lands, together with Bohemia, Moravia and Silesia, into an economically and socially prosperous whole – even, perhaps, in drawing Hungary into an effective Central-European community distinguished by religious toleration and

building of a medieval town under Habsburg rule. The site, on a hill, with a commanding view, and the central [posi]tion of the fortress castle, reflect the perpetual aggressive and defensive warfare in which the early [Hab]sburgs engaged.

Count Rudolph of Habsburg, King of the Germans, first of the dynasty to be elected to this office (1273). He was never crowned Emperor in Rome despite his policy of peaceful relations with Pope Gregory X. Painted on glass in St. Stephen's Cathedral, Vienna.

young Maximilian, son of the unhappy Frederick III, was his father's
y triumph.

entry of Charles, later Emperor Charles V, in Bruges.

Having reduced Pope Clement VII to vassalage Charles organised his own coronation, at Clement's hands, in Bologna in 1530. Rome lay in ruins and Charles was the last Emperor to be crowned by a Pope.

Philip II inherited from his father, Charles V, the throne Spain, and from his education in the Escorial, the prou Spanish, courtly manner.

The Thirty Years' War raged across the German lands and beyond, inflicting wounds which warped the social development of Central Europe for centuries afterwards.

The painting by Geffels of the relief of Vienna and the destruction of the Turkish host.

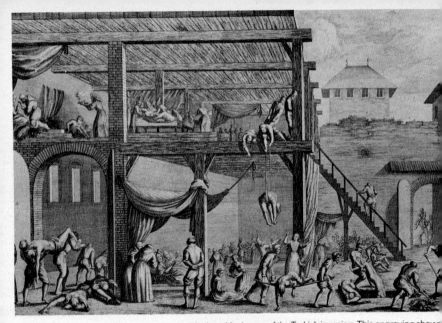

The Viennese suffered plague as well as siege in the critical years of the Turkish invasion. This engraving shows a hospital during the terrible epidemic of 1679.

Emperor Charles VI, affecting as always, the grand clothes and man of the Spanish court, in keeping with his lost throne of Spain.

Archduchess Maria Theresa before her accession to the throne of Austria at twenty-three.

Emperor Joseph II with his brother Archduke Ferdinand, painted by Batoni in 1769. Joseph became Emperor and co-Regent with his mother, after his father's death in 1765.

...eror Francis I riding with his queen, the Bavarian princess, Caroline Augusta.

...allied troops enter Paris in 1814, Emperors Alexander and Frederick William at their head. The Austrian ...aver of this scene insists that the French people were overjoyed to see them and that shouts of 'Long live ...llies' rose on every side.

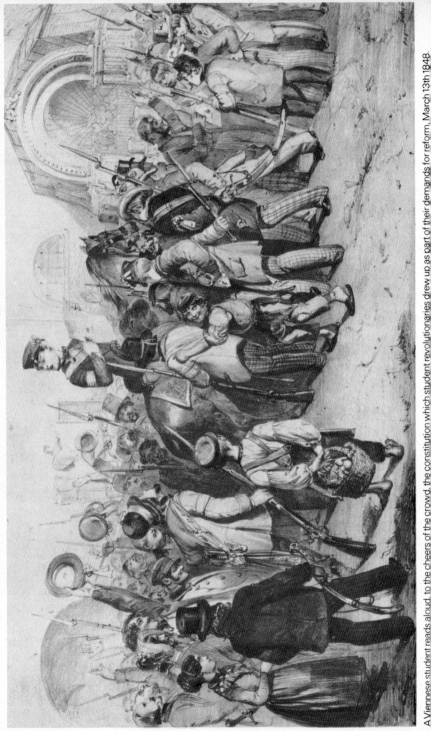

A Viennese student reads aloud, to the cheers of the crowd, the constitution which student revolutionaries drew up as part of their demands for reform, March 13th 1848.

March 17th 1848, the national flag is hauled up by Italian rebels in St. Mark's square Venice.

The National Guard fires on the Viennese rebels.

Cartoonists image of the National Guard during the uprising in Vienna.

A cartoon in *Punch* called 'Dropping the Pilot' mirrored public reaction to the decision of the young Kaiser William II to dismiss Bismark.

The state car in which Francis Ferdinand and his wife drove through the streets of Sarajevo. A few minutes later they were assasinated.

The lying in state of the Habsburg heir, and his wife Sophie Chotek.

enlightened institutions. He would have had to exercise extreme sureness of touch and tact in curbing the pretensions of the great territorial magnates and diminishing the particularism of the Estates of the various lands. But he had the imagination and the force of character to achieve all these things, provided he kept out of unnecessary wars. The only necessary war would have been occasioned, as it was, by the need to push the Turks far back into the Balkans – as, indeed, was done under Charles VI when, in 1717, Prince Eugene crowned his career with the capture of Belgrade.

Charles, alas, had none of his brother's qualities. He was much nicer and more human as a man than the pompous solemnity of his outward appearance could suggest. Like so many Habsburg emperors he was passionate for music, a good friend, a loving father. He had dignity in adversity (but it was an adversity he himself invited) and he could make a good joke on his death-bed. He would have been a useful master of a going concern. But Habsburg Austria was not yet a going concern; and it called for a great deal of constructive imagination to turn it into one. In so far as Charles was imaginative at all, he was afraid of the dark. The loss of Spain was a traumatic experience from which he never recovered. He had travelled from Barcelona to Vienna when his brother died so suddenly, promising to be back very soon, and leaving his young Brunswick wife as his regent. He was never to go back, but he went on behaving like a Spanish king, emphasizing the Spanish ceremonial which had distinguished his father's court, surrounding himself with advisers who also believed that Spain was what mattered most in the world, and finally, when he was forced to recognize that Spain was lost for ever, embarking on the construction of the immense monastic palace of Klosterneuburg attached to an ancient Augustine foundation on the Danube just above Vienna. Never finished, it was to be the Austrian Escorial – a palace, a retreat, a mausoleum, its great copper domes surmounted by huge replicas of the Imperial crown and the Austrian Archducal hat.

As for the dark, it was all around him. Charles was one of those men, not without ability, who are incapable of taking life as it comes and trusting themselves, their vitality, their instinct, their brains, their luck, to rise to an occasion when required to do so. In part, no doubt, because he had seen his brother die leaving no son behind him, in part because he had been so deeply shocked and affronted by his own loss of Spain, an object-lesson in the accidents that can beset humanity in its most exalted manifestations and in the precariousness of the tenure of kings, he allowed himself at a very early age to become obsessed with the need to secure the hereditary lands beyond challenge for his own issue, his daughter if he had no son. There was much sense in this. The lands were various and scattered and heaven knew who might not put forward a plausible claim to any part of them if sudden death removed their present monarch from the scene. More particularly, Joseph had had two daughters: if either one of them survived to marry, she and her husband, whoever he might be, would be senior to any daughter of Charles. So instead of concentrating all his energies on unifying his own lands and developing their economies, on building up a central army to intimidate all future aggressors, Charles from the very outset of his reign concentrated in a worrying kind of way on the self-appointed task of bribing the European powers, friends and enemies alike, into pledging themselves to recognize the integrity of the Habsburg inheritance in its entirety and the sovereignty of his, Charles's, designated successor. Above all at a moment of history at which every ruler, uninhibited by Imperial, religious or family loyalties, was unashamedly on the make, the powers, as might be expected, made the pledges, which cost them nothing, took the bribes, which cost Austria a good deal, and, when the time came, cheerfully broke the pledges.

His great device, the barren fruit of so much elaborate diplomacy, was the Pragmatic Sanction of 1713. If Charles had accompanied his costly efforts to get the Pragmatic Sanction recognized with a sensible policy towards Spain, with a conciliatory attitude towards his established allies, the Maritime Powers, with a firmly correct attitude elsewhere, and with administrative reform and financial retrenchment at home, the operation would have been worthwhile. With his aloof pomposity, his slow-moving mind cautious to the point of timidity, he would have lived in memory as the great consolidator, with a bee in his bonnet about security and a weakness for written agreements, eccentric, even dangerous, in an age distinguished for perfidy and greed. But he was hopelessly inconsistent. While devoting a great part of his energies to the search for ultimate security, again and again he threw security to the winds. His dream of returning to Spain in glory, or at least of obtaining a controlling interest in her affairs, alienated him from his old allies, England and Holland, and led him into a damaging war with France. His pursuit of recognition for his Pragmatic Sanction by Saxony was the direct cause of his unhappy participation in the War of the Polish Succession. His determination to compensate in the East for his losses in Italy arising from the conflict with France, together with his desire to prove his goodwill towards Russia, only lately emerged on to the international stage, drove him into an unnecessary war with Turkey in which he not only threw away the most valuable of Eugene's conquests but also achieved the ruin of his own army and the virtual bankruptcy of his realm.

It was the saddest story of a decent but mediocre ruler mistaking himself for a great statesman and war-leader, and sustained in this course in the teeth of the advice, the urgings, of the most gifted counsellor of the age, Prince Eugene, by a collection of silly, vain, ignorant and frequently corrupt place-men. All of them thought of Spain in terms already a century out of date; all of them underrated France's powers of recovery; none of them possessed the least understanding of England and the supreme importance to Austria of sustaining the closest alliance with that great maritime power; all were consumed with jealous hatred of Eugene, and encouraged the Emperor in his own uneasy jealousy of a superior mind.

Meanwhile Vienna was blossoming into a splendid capital. The great noble families vied with each other in the splendour of their town palaces within the walls, and the still greater magnificence of their summer palaces going up outside; the Hofburg was remodelled and the Fischers, father and son, built the marvellous Court Library and the Spanish Riding School; Eugene built for himself the Belvedere Palace, more royal than royal, on a hill which dominated the city; the Emperor poured vast sums into Fischer's masterpiece, the Karlskirche, a thanksgiving for deliverance from the plague and a glorification of himself; still completely under

Italian influence, the foundations of Vienna's great musical tradition were being laid – all presided over actively by poor Charles, who also delighted in mounting baroque operas and masquerades of the most spectacular and extravagant kind. And while all this was happening the affairs of the realm established by Ferdinand II, husbanded by Ferdinand III, triumphant under Leopold I, launched on a course of rationalization and internal expansion in the spirit of the age by Joseph I, were brought, if not to ruin, to the very edge of it. But not even in the direst financial straits did Charles abate the splendour of his court (which directly employed some 40,000 souls), the magnificence of his entertainments, or his insatiable passion for hunting at no matter what cost to the unfortunate peasants, whose crops were ravaged by his fanatically protected game.

In the end Charles's worst fears were realized: he left no son. What he did not know was that his daughter, Maria Theresa, at twenty-three, untrained, unaided, hampered by her father's frivolous and useless advisers, married to a Prince of Lorraine, Francis Stephen, amiable and kind but ungifted either as a soldier or a statesman, was to take hold of bankruptcy and chaos and, in the teeth of violent aggression on the part of half Europe, carry her inheritance from the verge of dissolution into the modern age.

7

The making of modern Austria:
Maria Theresa

THE young queen had no money, no army, virtually no central administration; worse still, no sensible advisers. At twenty-three, untrained, armed only with her beauty, her youth, her trust in God, and a character the strength of which neither she nor anybody else could yet appreciate, she stood at the head of a bankrupt empire, or collection of lands, which her father had brought to the edge of ruin. When she was acquainted by one of her elderly ministers with the true state of the realm she behaved with perfect calm and self-possession; but afterwards, alone with her favourite lady-in-waiting, she burst into tears.

She still did not know the half of it. The state of Austria would have been bad enough had the neighbouring powers been peacefully inclined: in fact they were wolves. It was not simply that France and Spain and Prussia were, unknown to her, maturing plans for the dismembering of the Empire whose integrity they were pledged by the Pragmatic Sanction to respect and uphold. Her own personal succession was soon to be challenged, and by her cousin, Charles Albert of Bavaria, who found plenty of support among her subjects: she was made the victim here not only of the discontent aroused by the disastrous policies of her father's last years, but also of the widespread distrust of her husband, who was erroneously regarded as a creature of the French. In fact the real creature of the French was Charles Albert of Bavaria himself, who was soon to be used by Versailles as the spearhead of a very determined attempt to shatter the power of Austria for ever.

The first blow, however, was to come out of a clear sky from a completely unexpected quarter. It was to come from Berlin. And it was to be the opening move in the career of the young King

Frederick II of Prussia which was to launch his country on her long course of aggrandizement, to destroy the old balance of power in Europe, and to establish Frederick as the greatest soldier of the age.

Frederick was barely four years older than Maria Theresa. He had been on the throne less than six months before her own accession. Nobody took him very seriously. He was the young prince who had quarrelled almost fatally with his brute of a father, been imprisoned, then sentenced to death after a vain attempt at escape, reprieved, but compelled to watch from his prison window the execution of a close friend. After that traumatic experience he had shut himself up in his castle at Rheinsberg and spent his days turning himself into a philosopher prince, scribbling bad verse, developing into an accomplished flautist, composing works on the theory of politics, turning his back on all things German, exalting French culture and cultivating the friendship of Voltaire, who flattered him outrageously. What nobody suspected was that this misleading young man, atheistic, homosexual, a founder-member of the Age of Reason, was also bent on personal glory and nursing plans for the aggrandizement of his barren, scattered kingdom. His father had a passion for military show. He had developed and trained to perfection a formidable fighting force. But he was aware of Prussia's limitations, and he loved his special regiment of giant grenadiers far too much to risk it in battle. Frederick, who appeared to be the least military-minded prince in Europe, had no such inhibitions: soldiers were made to be used. He was also a gambler, though the most long-headed man who ever staked a card or an army. He was also totally without scruple and regarded treachery as an arm of diplomacy and war. Finally, though this fact took a long time to emerge, he was a genius.

It was Maria Theresa's special fate to have been born into the same generation as this Frederick, who smiled while he struck and found nothing but joy in the marvellous turn of events, as it appeared to him, which, by placing Austria in the hands of an inexperienced girl surrounded by feeble and incompetent advisers, had delivered her into his hands. Never was any aggressor to pay more dearly for the most natural mistake in the world. The young girl, diffident, gay, warm-hearted, devout, the perfect adornment of the dawning rococo age, turned out to be steel. Nothing could have been more unfair. The swift little campaign on which the King of Prussia so confidently embarked in December 1740 was to condemn him to a lifetime of often desperate fighting at ruinous expense in blood and treasure. Before it was all over, more than twenty years later and after two long-drawn-out wars, Prussia itself was to be on the verge of total extinction, saved only by what must have seemed the miraculous death of his determined foe, Elisabeth of Russia – another of those major accidents of history. But saved it was, to emerge greater than before, and with Frederick II now Frederick the Great.

That first swift little campaign was severely limited in intention. Frederick was not a megalomaniac. Knowing that other powers, above all France, had wide-ranging designs on Austria, he determined to get in first and detach for himself the most valuable of all the Austrian provinces, Silesia, with its flourishing agriculture and rich mineral wealth which was conveniently adjacent to Prussia. He struck under cover of 'a cloak of darkness' even while he flattered Maria Theresa with fair words. He struck within three months of the young queen's accession, when Austria was totally unprepared, her palsied ministers full of fears as to what Bavaria and Spain might do and looking for a sign from France. He brought nearly thirty thousand of the best-trained soldiers in the world, as yet unblooded, against six thousand Austrians. There was no pitched battle. There could be no such thing. The Austrian commander, a magnificent soldier of Irish extraction called Maximilian von Browne, did well to keep his own forces intact and ready to strike again.

The young queen was more outraged than cast down by this act of highway robbery. She had freed from prison the generals condemned by her father for their failure against the Turks. One of these, Neipperg, a favourite of her husband's, was made commander-in-chief: it would be his task to form a new army and drive the Prussians out of Silesia in the spring. Maria Theresa had not the slightest doubt that this would happen. She also counted on the active support of England, pledged to uphold the Pragmatic Sanction and to supply her with money and troops. All too soon she was to discover that her commander-in-chief was no more equal to his job than her political advisers. The first head-on clash with Prussia came at Mollwitz in Bohemia in April 1741. It was a close-run thing. Frederick himself was convinced he had lost the battle and galloped off to save himself when the Austrian cavalry overwhelmed the Prussian horse. But he ran too soon. When all seemed lost it was discovered through the smoke that the Prussian infantry, in their dark blue uniforms, were still standing like a wall. A brand new military force, drilled with precision, equipped to the last button but hitherto untried, was making its *début* on the European battlefield which it was to dominate for the next two hundred years.

At the same time Maria Theresa found that England was a reluctant ally, anxious to preserve Austria as a counterpoise to France, but not at all interested in fighting to save her a province. In particular, George II feared that by antagonizing Frederick he would lay his beloved Hanover wide open to invasion by the Prussians. In general, the London government wished at all costs to avert the danger of a continental war involving a major collision with France.

But France was already on the war-path. The fire-eating soldier, Belle-Isle, thirsting for glory, had managed to convince the aged Cardinal Fleury and his soft-living master, Louis XV, that the time had come to shatter Austria and dismember her. Prussia had begun the process. France must quickly profit by it. The plan was to give active support to Charles Albert of Bavaria, moving swiftly down the Danube valley to take first Linz, then Vienna. There would soon be nothing left but the rump of Austria, the old hereditary lands. Charles Albert would be Emperor. There would be a greater Bavaria, a greater Saxony. Spain and Sardinia would take parts of Italy. There would be a greater Prussia too. But Belle-Isle did not fear this. There would be no dominant power in Central Europe, and French diplomacy would see to it that no dangerous combination would arise to challenge French hegemony. Then, supreme and unchallenged on the Continent, with no powerful foe at her back, France would be free to settle accounts with England once and for all, and sweep her from the seas.

These were the stakes. It was a wonderful dream. But it was never to be fulfilled. It was shattered by the courage and fighting spirit of a twenty-four-year-old queen, with no visible resources, with no talented and experienced adviser at her elbow, standing alone. Somehow, commanding, pleading, cajoling, exhorting, she was to infuse into her inherited advisers something of her own unbreakable will. She was fighting first for Silesia, which she was never to regain; then to keep the French and the Bavarians out of Vienna, then to drive them out of Prague, then to shatter the Spaniards and the French in Italy. She was fighting for her inheritance and for justice. She had not the slightest idea of the range and scope of the conflict which was to develop from the simple idea of resistance to an insolent and treacherous invader. The War of the Austrian Succession (1740–48) was seen by her above all as a war for Silesia. The Seven Years War (1756–63) was for her, above all, a war for the recovery of Silesia. The supreme enemy throughout was the Prussian, Frederick. But in fact both wars were stages in a cataclysmic process, ranging from Canada to Poland, from Italy to the Netherlands, from the Rhine to Bengal, in the course of which England was to establish her vast maritime empire at the expense of the French, while Austria was to be welded into a coherent and stable power.

Maria Theresa had neither the temperament nor the understanding to see this conflict for what it was (she was not alone in this). Neither had she the time. She lived from hand to mouth, from day to day. The enemy under her eyes was all she cared about, and she drove her generals on, urging them in effect to break out of the conventions of eighteenth-century warfare, with its stately manoeuvring, its copybook sieges, and be swift, unexpected, ruthless. She had in those early days, apart from Browne, one very good general, Khevenhüller. When Khevenhüller went into action against the Franco-Bavarians and was going on to take Munich, at a moment when things seemed desperate as never before, she wrote to him in terms most characteristic of the girl who still preferred to plead rather than command. With the letter went a portrait of herself and the infant Joseph:

Dear and faithful Khevenhüller – Here you behold the

Queen who knows what it is to be forsaken by the whole world. And here also is the heir to her throne. What do you think will become of this child? To you, as a true and tried servant of the State, your most gracious lady offers this picture of herself, and therewith her whole power and resources – everything, indeed, that her kingdom contains and can do ... May your achievements be as renowned as those of your master, the great Eugene, who rests in God.

But she could also command, and came increasingly to do so. After Mollwitz in April 1741 she had no choice but to reach what she regarded as a very temporary accommodation with Frederick, threatened as she now was by France, Bavaria, Saxony and Spain. Frederick himself was only too pleased to fall out of the struggle and digest his loot, leaving his new allies to keep up the pressure. The young queen's first great independent action was her celebrated appeal to the Hungarians in the summer of that year while the Bavarians were advancing on Vienna.

It was a brave action, made in the teeth of her German advisers. The Hungarians, as usual, were in a ferment of revolt. Maria Theresa, who had made a grand entry into Pressburg for her coronation, very quickly decided that the only hope for the future was to get these volatile and turbulent Hungarians, stubbornly clinging to their rights and always striving to exceed them, on her side. Since they could not be attached to her by force she determined to win them over by a calculated appeal to their chivalry and to their national pride. She would treat them as equal partners instead of as a subject people. She would throw herself on their mercy and appeal to their force of arms. And this, in a memorable scene before the grand assembly of the two houses of the Hungarian parliament or Diet, she did:

The very existence of the Kingdom of Hungary, of our own person, of our children, and our crown, are now at stake. Forsaken by all, we place our sole resource in the fidelity, arms and long-tried valour of the Hungarians. . . .

The Hungarians responded. They had no intention of transforming themselves into the obedient subjects of a Habsburg; but now that a Habsburg, and a beautiful woman in distress into the bargain, had for the first time in their history offered them the promise of a compact, they would work and fight with her for the fulfilment of that compact. They consecrated themselves to her service with their blood. It was not to amount to a great deal in practice, but it was enough to turn the day. For Hungary things would never be the same again. They would never be the same again for Maria Theresa either. She had been on the throne for less than a year. Throughout all that time she had behaved with the greatest diffidence towards her ancient advisers. Now she had broken away. She had felt her own power to inspire loyalty, devotion and the fighting spirit. She was now in command, and would stay there. She was soon to show that she could be hard and ruthless as well as pleading. Already she was ignoring the timorous and decrepit and making what she could of the tougher spirits around her. These were few and far between, and even here she first had to overcome the fundamental disloyalty and selfishness of a nobility which owed everything to her family and gave all too little in return. In one of these, the immensely rich Prince Kinsky, who was in charge of Bohemia and who had earlier tried to side-track the Prussian war because he feared for his own estates, she put her especial trust, although he was one of the most arrogant and difficult of men. It was only a month after the Hungarian apotheosis that the Bavarians and the Saxons and the French were to capture Prague – and Frederick, fearing of losing Silesia to this powerful coalition, came back into the fight. Everyone, her husband included, now a failed general, was in despair. But the young queen wrote to Kinsky:

So Prague is lost ...
Here, then, Kinsky, we find ourselves at the sticking point where only courage can save the country and the Queen. For without the country I should indeed be a poor princess. My own resolve is taken: to stake everything, win or lose, on saving Bohemia ... It may involve destruction and desolation which twenty years will be insufficient to restore; but I must hold the country and the soil, and for this all my armies, all the

Hungarians, shall die before I surrender an inch of it ... You will say that I am cruel; that is true. But I know that all the cruelties I commit today to hold the country, I shall one day be in a position to make good a hundred-fold. And this I shall do. But for the present I close my heart to pity. I rely on you ...

She was still only twenty-four. She was still the girl who could write to Francis that she felt uneasy 'like a little dog' when he was far away. But she was already emerging as one of the greatest rulers in history and the founder of modern Austria.

It may seem odd to start writing in these terms of a brilliant reign which was to give its name to an epoch and sing down the ages, a peak of elegance and extravagance, as the rococo emerged from the baroque and then carried feeling to the threshold of romanticism. But it was from incessant and tortuous diplomacy, the desperate struggle for survival in an age of total cynicism among rulers, that Theresian Austria emerged.

During the course of that first war in which the French fought initially as the nominal auxiliaries of Bavaria, the English as auxiliaries of Austria, there were violent swings of fortune. The French were driven out of Prague, should have been destroyed, but made an epic winter march across Europe, losing thousands but keeping their guns. Charles Albert of Bavaria was crowned King of Bohemia, then elected Emperor. But on the day of his election the Austrians took his own capital, Munich. The Austrians did well against the Spaniards in Italy. Browne advanced deep into Provence. The English, active at last, won the battle of Dettingen by the skin of their teeth in 1743, but were soon thrown into confusion by the 1745 rebellion when Charles Edward Stuart, helped by the French, set up his standard in Scotland and remained a dangerous threat until Culloden a year later. Also in 1745 came the overruning of the Austrian Netherlands by the brilliant Marshal Saxe winning a resounding victory at Fontenoy. Frederick fell out of the struggle in 1742 with the Treaty of Breslau; he was soon back and fighting hard until the Treaty of Dresden, signed on Christmas Day 1745, allowed him to vanish again with Silesia under his belt. Maria Theresa went on fighting.

There was a moment when she dreamed of an annihilating victory. Already in 1743 she had been able to journey to Prague for her coronation as Queen of Bohemia. In September 1745 she achieved a devouring ambition. Charles Albert had died prematurely in January. The Imperial crown was up for auction again. This time she obtained it for her husband. Francis became Emperor.

But there was no annihilating victory. The dream of recovering Alsace and Lorraine, of capturing Naples, vanished as the indeterminate battles swung to and fro. At last, in 1748, even Maria Theresa was ready for peace. The treaty was signed at Aix-la-Chapelle. On the face of it the war need never have been fought. Frederick had Silesia, France gained nothing. England relinquished her colonial conquests . . . But in fact what the war had done for Maria Theresa was to teach her the grammar of politics, diplomacy and administration – to teach her also to know herself. She was thirty-one. For some years she had realized that what Austria needed for survival was root-and-branch reform. She had already been taking measures to this end. Now, for eight years, she was to work at the task of turning her inheritance into a centralized power.

Her vitality, gaiety and vigour were fantastic. Even while she fought her bitter war she found time to produce five more children. First the long-awaited heir, Joseph, with whom she was pregnant when her father died. Then two girls and two boys, one of whom died young. There were still seven more to come, sixteen in all. She was determined to be a good wife to her husband and demanded much of him as a husband in return, regarding his inconsistencies with a jealous eye, being so carried away, indeed, by her detestation of marital infidelity (here she was quite at odds with her time) that she took it out on her subjects, even to the extent of establishing a ludicrous institution nicknamed 'the Chastity Commission', designed to hunt down and punish ladies whose sexual morals did not measure up to her high standards. In this and in this alone, she was absurd. For the rest, until she began to feel the burden of the years, she was gaiety itself. Throughout this first long period of strain she enjoyed her dancing, her card-playing, festivities of every kind; and even while she was fighting half Europe and finding it extremely difficult to scrape together enough money to keep her army paid, her thoughts were turning, in a truly eighteenth-century manner, to the building of the immense, beautiful and madly extravagant summer palace at Schönbrunn with its 1,400 rooms, which was to be her favourite home. When the English complained because, they said, she was squandering their subsidies on an architectural show-piece instead of using them to provide the sinews of war, she could reply, in perfect good faith, that she was doing nothing of the kind: *all* the subsidies went on the war; to build Schönbrunn she borrowed from the Jews. . . .

Looking back to those early days it is almost impossible to see how this inexperienced, untrained, fundamentally diffident young woman managed. A clue to her strength of character and common sense amounting to genius is to be found in the way she held off her senior advisers with one hand while searching out and finding new men: once they were found she could sometimes relax.

The first of these, who was to take the place of a father, she found very quickly in the son of a house of Portuguese grandees, long in the Austrian service. Don Manuel Telles de Menezes e Castro, Count Tarouca, later created Duke of Silva. He was a shrewd and gifted diplomat, wise and relaxed. He was appalled when his monarch soon after her accession said she wished him to serve at her side, to tell her the truth about all things hidden from her by the flattery of others and her own self-will, 'to show me my faults and make me recognize them. . . . This being most necessary for a ruler, since there are few or none at all to be found who will do this, commonly refraining out of awe or self-interest.' But he took the job on, kept at it for years, and although he frequently disagreed with the policies of his royal mistress and her other advisers, and although surrounded by jealous and intriguing courtiers, he kept her confidence for thirty years until he died. At first his prime concern was to curb the young queen's high spirits, to help her to organize her days and prevent her from wasting her energies on too much detailed work by day and too much revelry by night. Later, when her immense successes began to turn to dust and ashes in her mouth, it was he who kept her from despair at the futility of worldly action, urging her to relax and try to recapture the enjoyments of her early days. Always he acted as a sort of secular father confessor and did a great deal to subdue the tendency to high-handed arrogance which developed in middle age with the discovery that she was incomparably the most competent figure in her own realm and the one who could get things done most expeditiously and best. Second only to her own good sense and fundamental humility, she owed to him the fact that she went on growing and came through the period when she might have hardened and coarsened into the pattern of a proud and demanding monarch to rediscover her true self. It was an extraordinary relationship. The young Queen Victoria leaned on Melbourne; but Tarouca was a Melbourne without power, and Maria Theresa continued to lean on him until his death.

The next man she picked was her body-doctor and personal physician, whom she made Court Librarian and the head of the Vienna Medical school, the Dutchman, Gerhard van Swieten. He was not the best of doctors (who, in those days, was?), but he was a great man and a polymath, and he was to turn the Vienna Medical School into a model for Europe. A pupil of the founder of modern medicine, Boorhave of Leyden, he earned Maria Theresa's gratitude by his treatment of her dearly loved sister, Marianne, who was married to her brother-in-law, Charles of Lorraine, Governor of the Netherlands. Marianne in fact died but, characteristically, once she had given her trust to Van Swieten, the Empress did not withdraw it. She brought him down to Vienna, established him in the teeth of violent opposition from the Austrian medicos and others, stood by him in all the violent controversies which inevitably surround an outsider of genius who sets out to revolutionize the existing state of affairs. Van Swieten soon became a major influence in Maria Theresa's life. If Tarouca was her conscience, Van Swieten was her guide and support as Austria groped its way into the Enlightenment. The Empress herself had no sympathy at all for abstract ideas, for philosophy of any kind. Unthinkingly devout, firm in her ancient faith, she recoiled with all her being from the vanities of the Age of Reason. Her instinct was to leave all affairs of the mind to the church, above all to her beloved Jesuits. Van Swieten was detested and abhorred by the churchmen

III

because, though a good Catholic, he was scientific in his approach and open in his ideas. By encouraging him and protecting him, Maria Theresa was actively undermining the very ground on which she stood. By making him Court Librarian first, then the chief censor, she was opening her lands to the new thought from which she shrank. This illustrates another aspect of her character: it was as though she understood the need for new ideas. Even though she herself must refuse to entertain them, through Van Swieten she gave them house-room and enabled them to grow.

The third great man she chose was Wilhelm, Count Haugwitz, an unprepossessing man of great courage, tenacity and practical vision. It was his task to turn a ramshackle collection of feudal lands into a relatively centralized power. Maria Theresa was not in the least attracted by reform for its own sake. But just as she had seen in the first days of her reign that sooner or later she would have to find better ministers and advisers than the ones she had inherited from her father, so she soon came to see that if Austria were to survive she would have to bring to heel the men who had helped to ruin it and to reform the institutions which denied her effective power. The men were the great nobles and magnates who owed everything to her ancestors and gave precious little in return, running their vast territories like petty monarchs, paying no taxes, contributing what it suited them to contribute in times of war (a few contributed much in men and treasure: most did not). The institutions were, above all, the various Estates, which legislated for their own local, national and provincial interests without a thought outside them. The young queen saw that the first thing she needed was a standing army on which she could rely and which must be regularly paid. To pay for it the rich must be taxed. To achieve this end she needed a centralized bureaucracy. To ensure a supply of trained officers for her army and trained bureaucrats for her administration there had to be academies and schools. All this was applied common sense. But there was something added. This remarkable young woman, who knew nothing about soldiering, finance, administration, education, or the lives of the poor, this spendthrift girl, surrounded from birth by a wealthy and arrogant nobility, this devout Catholic with her unquestioning faith that the *status quo* had been ordained by God, felt in her bones that there was something deeply wrong with a system which treated the vast majority of her subjects, the peasants, as expendable, as cannon-fodder, as serfs. There were hidden talents, she was sure, to be discovered and nurtured: to treat the peasants as animals was wasteful. It was also, she decided, wrong, unjust, inequitable.

This was the ground on which Haugwitz was to operate. And to Maria Theresa's still cloudy intimations of efficiency, justice and humanity he brought administrative talent and deep experience. Ironically, he had acquired his experience governing the tiny rump of Silesia, and in Silesia he had had the opportunity to contemplate the workings of the Prussian military and social system, and the imagination to apply what he learnt to his own parish. Now, in the teeth of bitter resentment on the part of the great magnates, but under the fierce and passionate protection of his Empress, he was to apply them to the whole of Austria. Only Hungary with its special privileges remained outside the great range of his reforms.

He was not only a man of great steadiness, wisdom and tenacity of purpose; he was not only the first great civil servant and born administrator thrown up by the Habsburg Empire; he also understood economics as well as any European of that age (Adam Smith was twenty-three years his junior), and he had the supreme advantage, as governor of the rump of Silesia, of seeing the Prussian way of doing things close to.

The first thing he had to do was to put the army on a satisfactory footing. His plan called for a standing army at the immediate disposal of the Crown of 108,000 men. This was to cost fourteen million gulden out of a total revenue of forty million. The money was to come from taxes. Instead of supplying troops as and when they saw fit, the nobility, the Estates, the Lands, were to pay cash on a regular basis: the central government itself would then raise and control and pay the troops. The taxes were to be based on the value of the immovable property of every individual, this value to be determined by commissions of experts, or rating officers.

Income was calculated as being five per cent of the agreed capital value, and on this income, notional or real, the nobility had to pay one-hundredth part, the peasantry one-fiftieth.

This in itself was a wholly revolutionary idea. To the nobility it was inconceivable that they should have to pay taxes. The peasants had always been taxed. This was proper. But the nobility saw themselves as the men who ran the country on the Crown's behalf and provided for its defence in war. The peasants and the urban tradesmen owned their very existence to the protection of the feudal lords. For this it was right that they should pay. Now the protectors themselves were being asked to pay.

In the event they did pay – everywhere except Hungary: not even Maria Theresa could turn the Hungarian magnates into tax-payers. The rest paid reluctantly and with bitter complaining; but the principle was firmly established. There was tremendous uproar, but surprisingly little organized resistance. And very soon, with a real army firmly under her control, Maria Theresa was in a position to weld that army into a coherent striking force – that force which, gathering strength over the next century, was to develop into the main unifying element in a polyglot state – with Germans, Hungarians, Czechs, Poles, Slovaks, Rumanians, Italians, Slovenes, Croats and others besides all serving together and owing their first loyalty not to their own countries but to the Habsburg crown – 'Patriots for me', in the words of the later emperor, Francis II, who had no use for national patriotisms of any kind.

With the new army and the new cadet schools came a new kind of officer corps in which skill at arms was theoretically more important than antiquity of blood, though not always so in practice. Those nobles, like Prince Liechtenstein, who had already distinguished themselves by making voluntary contributions to past war efforts, now distinguished themselves no less under the new regime; and they were joined by professional soldiers like Daun, Laudon and Lacy, who were to make a better showing of Austrian arms in the next war when it came, the Seven Years War of 1756–63. Maria Theresa herself, always resenting the fact that her sex forbade her to assume command in the field, took an immense pride in her new army, frequently visiting the new permanent encampments and assisting at manoeuvres. Of course it was all much better on paper than in practice. When the test of war came it was quickly discovered that it took more than the Imperial signature to a decree drafted by Haugwitz to overcome the inertia of centuries. But the transformation was real; it was real enough, when the next test came, to make Frederick of Prussia exclaim: 'These are not the same old Austrians at all!'

With fiscal and military reforms came others. The administrations of the Austrian and Bohemian lands were merged and centralized. Education was developed to a remarkable degree and above all, at this stage, by the foundation of high schools and institutions for the training of army officers and civil servants. Most importantly, Haugwitz achieved at a stroke of the Empress's pen the formal separation of administration and the judiciary. And this great reform of 1749 was itself the signal for the drawing up of a new code of laws. Started in 1752, the work went on until 1766 when the *Codex Theresianus* defining civil rights was at last published, followed by the *Constitutio Criminalis* in 1778, which was to be the foundation of the model code of 1811, thirty-one years after the death of the reforming Empress.

The last great initiative of the still young queen was the discovery and elevation of her personal Disraeli, Wenzel Anton, Count Kaunitz-Rietberg, later Prince Kaunitz, who turned from the Church to make himself a career in politics, rose like a comet and sustained himself in orbit from 1753, when Maria Theresa made him her chancellor, until his death in 1794. Thus this brilliant hypochondriac, who always thought he was at death's door, survived his Empress by fourteen years and retained office through two more reigns and into a fourth. He was incomparably the most accomplished diplomat of his age, one of the most accomplished of all time; but whether his statesmanship was a match for his diplomatic skill, or whether the swiftness and clarity of his mind, the boldness of his decision-making, prevented him from giving proper weight to the imponderables of history is open to debate. As far as his Imperial mistress was concerned, for nearly thirty years he was her pathfinder through the maze of eighteenth-century power politics, the guide on whom she utterly relied. It was only towards the end of her reign that his image became a little tarnished. Then, working with her son and co-Regent, the Emperor Joseph II, he was to do his best to break her heart by deeply embroiling the Empire in the game of unscrupulous aggrandizement which Maria Theresa regarded as immoral and a betrayal of all she sought to stand for: the first partition of Poland and the farcical and disgraceful War of the Bavarian Succession.

He was unscrupulous from the beginning, but in 1744 when he first came to Maria Theresa's notice as a career official in the foreign service she did not see this. What she saw, at twenty-seven, was a diplomat only five years older than herself, forty years younger than her inherited advisers, who showed every sign of being ten times more able, more imaginative, more swift, more penetrating than all his seniors put together. He had an eye for the facts of power and knew how to exploit them. Better, he knew how to turn weakness into strength. He was also discreet and incorruptible in an age of indiscretion and corruption. His human failings, which were spectacular – his vanity, his hypochondria, his silliness about women – all counted for nothing beside his ability and his understanding of reality, in the eyes of the woman who had the strongest views in the world about such failings. She gave him her trust, his elaborate plan to reverse the traditional system of alliances secured for him her devotion.

Prussia had to be put down, Silesia with all its wealth regained. Kaunitz gave his Empress strong political arguments in support of her own heart's desire. He went on to show the only way in which it could be done. It meant a complete revolution in Austrian thinking; more than this, in the generally accepted basis of the European balance. Before the advent of Frederick of Prussia France had been the great enemy of Habsburg. She was still very much the enemy. England, the hereditary foe of France, was therefore Austria's natural ally. But England used Austria only as a convenience, to engage the French continental army while the English fleet manoeuvred and fought for command of the seas and for overseas empire. The succession war had proved that England would not lift a finger to win Silesia for Austria or to humble Prussia. She would only exert herself to meet an active threat from

France. To put the new Prussia down called for nothing less than a continental coalition. But with Austria and France at daggers drawn, with France, moreover, allied with Prussia, this could not be.

The idea that Austria might break with England, might ally herself with her ancient enemy, France, was simply not on the board. It never so much as crossed the minds of the men who made policy in London, in Paris, in St. Petersburg, in Berlin. In Vienna it was unheard-of and undreamt-of. It needed Kaunitz to think of it. And it needed Maria Theresa, feeling her own strength now, to say in effect: 'Very well. Go to Paris as my ambassador and see what you can do.'

Kaunitz went. He descended on Versailles with the richest imaginable retinue, entertained like a reigning prince, dazzled with his brilliance. For three years he took soundings. There was no question of a direct approach. All he could do was to present a smiling face, bury past bitterness, raise doubts about the good faith of Frederick – and make friends. In 1753 Maria Theresa recalled him from Paris with, on the face of it, nothing at all accomplished. She still had unbounded faith in him. She made him her chancellor and he used his power unhesitatingly and unobstructed by his Empress to bring all the threads of government together into his own hands. Foreign diplomats in Vienna hardly knew what to make of this man who had so far achieved nothing, whose manners and eccentricities were frivolous to a degree, a Voltairian, whose cynicism was a by-word, and who yet stood higher than any other in the estimation of an Imperial mistress whose character and views were diametrically opposed to his. But with all his playacting he could not conceal the formidable power of his intellect; and it soon became apparent that this went with strength of character, tenacity of purpose and almost infinite patience. For three more years he worked away at his great design, which involved keeping the lines open with the maritime powers while seeking to draw not only France, but Russia too, into his net. He had no choice but to wait on events; but sooner or later, he was convinced, England, or Prussia, or both, would make a false move and he would know how to profit from it. The false move came early in 1756.

It was made by England, over-anxious for the security of George II's precious Hanover in face of a largely hypothetical danger from France. Because her ally, Austria, would not pledge sufficient help in case of a threat to Hanover, Newcastle, then Prime Minister, decided to do a direct deal with Frederick of Prussia. Overnight Prussia was transformed in the eyes of Louis XV from an uneasy ally into a dangerous foe. Further, Russia, who had designs on East Prussia, also considered herself betrayed by England. The time had come for Kaunitz to make hay. If France would stay neutral in a defensive alliance with Austria, Austria would combine with Russia to shatter Frederick, and England would be impotent. In fact things turned out better than Kaunitz had ever allowed himself to dream. Louis XV had never liked Frederick. He now over-reacted sharply, partly to assert himself against his own pro-Prussian faction, more particularly because he was at that time profoundly under the influence of Madame de Pompadour, who fancied herself as a woman of state and whose confidence Kaunitz had successfully set himself to gain during his apparently barren years in Paris.

In no time at all the time-honoured pattern of European power was turned upside down. Austria, France and Russia stood against England, Holland and Prussia. It needed only a spark to set off a continental war. That spark was provided by Frederick, deeply apprehensive about the consequences of what was indeed a formidable encirclement: to make sure of Silesia and to open the way to an invasion of Bohemia in case of need, secretly, and without a declaration of war, he moved into Saxony on 29 August.

This was the overture to the Seven Years War. For Austria it began and ended as the third war for Silesia. Everything that occurred in the course of that grim and ruinous conflict was seen from Vienna in terms of the humiliation of Prussia and the recovery of Silesia. For England and for France it was a supreme crisis in the long-drawn-out struggle for maritime supremacy, for trade and overseas empire. When it was all over France was broken as a sea power and driven out of Canada and India. Austria was re-established as a coherent power, but she had lost Silesia for ever.

Russia had finally emerged as one of the main arbiters of Europe. Prussia, by the very act of her survival, had become a major power, by her very existence from then on frustrating Austria's claim to leadership in Germany.

That Prussia survived at all was due in the first place to the genius of Frederick who drove her to the limit and beyond. The myth of infallibility was shattered by his crushing defeat at Kolin in June 1757 by Maria Theresa's new commander, Leopold Daun. But though he fought back, and won brilliantly at Rossbach and Leuthen, in the autumn of 1758 at Hochkirch he was beaten again by Daun, working together with two even more able commanders, Laudon and Lacy. And then, in the summer of 1759, came shattering defeat at the hands of the Russians, working together with Laudon, at Kunersdorf. It looked like the beginning of the end. Properly concerted action between the Russians and the Austrians would have broken Frederick for ever: but those allies quarrelled among themselves, as allies do. The opportunity was lost. Even so, for the next three years Frederick kept going in what seemed a hopeless situation only by his immense drive, his resilience, his refusal to recognize defeat. He had been saved once by the defeat of the French at Minden, when English troops fought well under Ferdinand of Brunswick, and again and again by his own super-human exertions, which included not only spectacular victories over the Austrians at Torgau and Liegnitz but also innumerable evasive or spoiling actions that seemed inspired. By 1761 the French were virtually out of the fight, but Austria and Russia had still more men. The Prussian economy was ruined. Frederick himself was in a suicidal mood, seeking death on the battlefield. It seemed all up with him: nothing could prevent his final annihilation and the collapse of Prussia as an independent power. He was saved only by an act of God, by the death, on 5 January 1762, of the Tsaritsa Elisabeth who, from the beginning, had rivalled Maria Theresa herself in her determination to bring Frederick down. Elisabeth was succeeded by the young Tsar Peter III, a semi-imbecile, married to the German princess Catherine of Anhalt-Zerbst, later to be known as Catherine the Great. Peter had an obsessional admiration for Frederick of Prussia. He was to live and reign for only a few months before he was murdered by the palace guard with the connivance of his formidable young wife, later to shine as the Queen of the Enlightenment, the Semiramis of the North. His one positive act was to take Russia out of the war in the nick of time to save Frederick, thus ensuring the survival of the power which was later to unify Germany under the Prussian king and visit his own suffering country with cataclysmic punishment on a scale unprecedented in modern history.

Maria Theresa had had enough. This whole war had been out of character for her, and she knew it. Later she was to reproach herself bitterly for many sins of omission and commission, among them for 'having made war out of pride'. She had fought like a tiger in the War of the Succession: it had been forced on her and there was no other way to survive. At the outbreak of the Seven Years War she could tell herself, and did, that her action was no more than a legitimate and reasonable attempt to recover territory wrenched from her by force after an unprovoked and treacherous assault. This was true. The fact remained that the Seven Years War, although again technically started by Frederick, was from the point of view of Vienna the outcome of a carefully planned, ingeniously articulated plan which, as the day of its realization drew near, involved Maria Theresa, whose supreme qualities were her honesty and essential goodness, increasingly in equivocation and deception. At first she spoke truthfully in saying she had no intention of going to war to recover Silesia, that this was a task that might fall to her successor. But she went on saying this long after she had changed her mind, led on by Kaunitz and excited and dazzled by the boldness of his vision and attack. It is true that the lies she told and the disingenuousness of her self-justification to her English ally were venial when compared with the treacheries of which she herself had earlier been the victim. But this remarkable woman would demand to be judged by her own standards. Her own standards were high, far higher than those of any other contemporary ruler; and on the eve of the Seven Years War, impatient, fully aware now of her own great strength, grown a little arrogant in that strength, she fell below those standards. The remarkable thing is that she still had strength in reserve to recover from this coarsening of her character. She had been instrumental in spreading suffering, bloodshed and ruin on a major scale.

For the rest of her life – and she had another seventeen years to go after the Peace of Hubertusburg – she was determined never again to countenance war except in the desperation of self-defence.

8

Reforming despot: Joseph II

WHEN the Seven Years War began Maria Theresa was thirty-nine and at the summit of her powers. Two years after it ended, when she was still only forty-eight, her beloved husband died suddenly, and it was to her the end of the world. Nobody will ever know precisely what Francis came to mean for Maria Theresa. She had the very extraordinary gift which allowed her to see the shortcomings of those closest to her without in the least abating her affection. Thus in her very early days she discovered that Francis, whom she adored, was in no way a leader of men; he was irresolute, slow and excessively cautious, altogether lacking attack and flair, either as a commander in the field or as an adviser in the council-chamber. Soon, too, she found he was inconstant. But she bore him sixteen children, she put up with his infidelities and, while keeping him away from the army after a disastrous start, she encouraged his one great talent, which was for finance (he made her a great private fortune) and smiled on his amiable enthusiasm for the arts and sciences. Evidently, as the kindly father of her children and the one man with whom she could relax completely in private, he gave her all she needed. When he died she was shattered. She told her lady-in-waiting to cut off her superb golden hair. She went into mourning, and she was to wear nothing but black for the rest of her life. But although for a brief period she convinced herself that she would never again be good for anything, in fact the next fifteen years were to be years of very great activity, much of it highly beneficial. They were also to be heavily clouded by a never-ending conflict with her son and heir, for fifteen years her co-Regent, the Emperor Joseph II; and later by the scandalous behaviour of her youngest daughter, Maria Antonia, who at fifteen, in 1770, a living sacrifice to the new alliance with the

Bourbons, was married off to the French Dauphin as Marie-Antoinette.

Joseph was a difficult boy from the nursery onwards. He became a most difficult man. No ruler was ever more high-minded, none strove more single-mindedly to reform an antiquated system, none was readier to sacrifice his life, his treasure as well, to his peoples (he made over the whole of his father's vast fortune to the State); none was more modest in his personal life. But there was a fateful flaw. He was excessively self-willed. In his very modesty there was ostentation. His concern for the well-being of the poor arose largely from his dislike and contempt for the rich. His reforms, which were far-reaching, were in no way a response to the demands, explicit or unspoken, of his subjects: they were expressions of his own private ideas of what was good and proper. He and he alone knew what was best. He and he alone was Emperor. He was the archtype of the benevolent despot, far more autocratic than his mother had ever been. Worse, with all his real concern for the spiritual and material well-being of his subjects, with all his loathing of formality, protocol and showy extravagance, he harboured dreams of glory: unlike any of his Habsburg ancestors for centuries past, he thought in terms of territorial aggrandizement through war and was determined to prove himself as a brilliant commander in the field. He was not an atheist, far from it: he was a devout Catholic. But he also worshipped power, and he was deeply impressed and influenced by those two great virtuosi in the cynical use of power: Frederick the Great of Prussia, and Catherine the Great of Russia. He aspired to be Joseph the Great of Austria. He failed.

The pity of it was that he had so many good ideas. Maria Theresa, secure in the simplicities of her deep religious faith, was the least intellectual of rulers. Kaunitz might be a Voltairian, but he had the sense to keep his ideas to himself, patronizing men of ideas by stealth. Only Van Swieten was allowed to introduce the breath of the Enlightenment and stand up to his mistress's beloved Jesuits; but he had to go very carefully indeed and represent the new spirit of the times not at all in terms of theory, only in terms of practical statecraft. It is true that the great Empress had a passion for education; but education for her was essentially the means of turning out better and more useful citizens: abstract ideas were anathema to her. By 1765, when Joseph became co-Regent, it was high time in Vienna for a breath of stimulating air from Voltaire, from Diderot, from Montesquieu to blow away the cobwebs; and if Joseph had gone about his business quietly, humanely, above all tactfully, he would have been in a very strong position to open his mother's mind to the changing needs of the age. She was, remarkably, still growing. Dimly, she herself was aware of these needs – not intellectually, but through that sixth sense which told her what was necessary from a purely practical point of view, even though she might be revolted by the necessity. But tact was the last quality to look for in Joseph. Perhaps because his mother was all tact, perhaps because his father had so amiably been all things to all men, he not only lacked any vestige of tact, he actively despised it. He delighted in humiliating his opponents (there was a streak of sadism in him); towards his mother he alternated between almost abject outpourings of love and devotion and the presentation of his most radical ideas in the manner best calculated to outrage her in her deepest instincts. He hectored, he bullied, he harangued. He could not argue the need for brains in the civil service without jeering at his mother's aristocratic friends; but she was herself aware of the need and of the shortcomings of the great noble families, and had done much to curtail their powers. He could not plead for religious toleration (one of his mother's blindest spots; but she was ready to argue about it) without rushing headlong into collision with his mother's most sacred beliefs. He raved to her about the excellencies of her ancient enemy, Frederick, and the marvellous qualities of Catherine of Russia whom she regarded, not without cause, as a godless whore ... To complicate matters further, with all his outward austerity, his crisp matter-of-factness, his rudenesses and withering sarcasms, he was over-burdened with self-pity. The early death of his young bride, Isabella of Parma, intelligent, clever, highly cultivated, full of the most penetrating insights, enchanting and warm-hearted too, was a blow of the most shattering kind, and he was quite broken up by it. At the same time this tragic bereavement was seized upon by Joseph as a sort of licence to regard himself as the most ill-used person in the world.

He was twenty-four when his father died. The year before he had been crowned King of the Romans at Frankfurt, which meant that he automatically succeeded Francis as Emperor. For fifteen years, while professing profound filial love and total devotion, he was to be in incessant conflict with his mother. Time and time again he threatened abdication as co-Regent, time and time again Maria Theresa seemed on the verge of throwing in the sponge and giving her difficult son his head. Kaunitz, who actively sympathized with many of Joseph's ideas, found even his supreme diplomatic skill stretched to the limit as he manoeuvred incessantly between them. The common idea was that a boldly reforming and visionary young Emperor was being frustrated at every turn by a bigoted woman who rejected all new ideas out of hand. Nothing could be farther from the truth. Maria Theresa, though deeply conservative in her instincts, had been a boldly reforming monarch when Joseph was in the cradle. She continued revising her ideas, and many of the reforms of her last phase, attributed to Joseph, came from her – above all in the judiciary, in education, particularly the spectacular development of compulsory primary education, and in the improvement in the lot of the poor peasants. The concrete issues on which they actively disagreed were very few: apart from the matter of religious toleration, what caused Maria Theresa most grief was her son's propensity for territorial aggrandizement by *force majeure* or war. Her stubborn refusal to recognize any justification for this was the most shining virtue of her later years. When one examines the mass of letters and memoranda exchanged betwen them, a body of correspondence of enthralling interest and, on Maria Theresa's side, of extreme liveliness and verve, it becomes clear that the Empress's main anxiety was caused not by specific items of disagreement but by what she saw as potentially disastrous defects of character in her eldest son. Even when Joseph was in the nursery she was writing to his tutor about his rudeness, his arrogance towards his inferiors, his rejection of all criticism: 'He expects to be obeyed and honoured, finds criticism unpleasant, almost intolerable, indeed, gives way to all his own whims, but behaves discourteously, even rudely to others.' Above all she was distressed by 'the pleasure he is prone to have in seizing on the shortcomings, physical or otherwise, of others and pouring ridicule on them .. a failing especially reprehensible in the great, who can so easily hurt or embarrass those who cannot defend themselves.'

And so it went on. Twenty years later she was driven to write directly to her son, Emperor and co-Regent now, with the same sort of complaint:

Do you honestly imagine that you can keep faithful servants by behaving in this manner? I fear very much that you will become the tool of rascals who, to achieve their own ends, will put up with treatment from you of a kind that no truly devoted soul could tolerate ... But what hurts me most of all was that you spoke as you did, not in sudden anger ... that is to say, you decided after full reflection to plant a dagger in the hearts of men whom you yourself regard most highly ... with your sarcasm and exaggerated reproaches ... And it is not the Emperor, not the co-Regent who utters such biting sarcastic, ugly words: they come from the heart of Joseph. It is this that fills me with alarm, it is this which will spell the wreck of your own life and the downfall of the monarchy and all of us ...

The monarchy in fact survived for a century and a half to come. It is conceivable, but improbable, that it would have survived to the present day as a constitutional monarchy holding together a supranational state had Joseph II shared the qualities of his grand-uncle, Joseph I, or his mother. But Joseph's own life was indeed wrecked, as Maria Theresa foresaw. She was not negligible as a prophet. Thus, for example, in 1775, five years before her death, appealing to her youngest daughter, Marie-Antoinette, now Queen of France, begging her to try to behave more sensibly, she wrote: 'Your luck can all too easily change, and by your own fault you may well find yourself plunged into deepest misery ... One day you will recognize the truth of this, but then it will be too late.'

Joseph's life was wrecked because he had no sense whatsoever of the sentiments and emotions governing human behaviour. He thought he could put his world to rights by decree, riding rough-shod over the traditional leaders of society and regimenting the common people and the peasants. He alone knew what was best for them, and he alone could order it. During the fifteen years of his co-regency his mother, at the cost of immense expenditure of nervous energy, managed to curb his natural despotism in the domestic sphere, but the moment she was dead decree followed decree – some good, some downright bad, some ludicrous, none properly thought through – in dizzy succession. There was no consistency, no broad view, no weighing of the consequences, no consultation of established interest; it was enough for Joseph to think up a new idea; next day it was law. He abolished serfdom, he broke the power of the Church, suppressing large numbers of rich foundations and diverting their treasure to the common good, he strengthened the bureaucracy established by his mother, he put an end to imperial extravagance and went about among the people unassumingly dressed. All these things were good. All were done in the wrong way, the way calculated to be offensive to the greatest number. As an example, he alienated the Bohemians by imposing on them a bureaucracy composed almost exclusively of Germans – not because he favoured the Germans but because he considered them more efficient. And so on. With the result that before his death all his peoples were simmering with revolt and some, notably in the Netherlands, were up in arms against him. He had meant so well. He had received, in return, nothing but black ingratitude. When he died, after ten years of individual rule, the throne was tottering and poor Joseph in his bitterness left an epitaph to be carved on his tomb: 'Here lies Joseph II, who failed in everything he undertook.'

He failed in other ways too, even while his mother lived, and in the teeth of sustained and impassioned protests on her part. Russia had made her formal entry as a great power on to the main international stage as Austria's ally in the Seven Years War, introducing a new, imponderable factor into the European power game. Under Catherine the Great she had at last succeeded in establishing herself on the Black Sea. She then set about reducing Poland. In 1772 Catherine and Maria Theresa's detested foe, Frederick of Prussia, came together to carve up Poland for their own advantage and sought to make Austria an accessory in this crime. Maria Theresa was outraged. She was being invited to benefit by an act of cold-blooded aggression of precisely the kind that

Frederick had committed in Silesia thirty years earlier. But Joseph, now backed by Kaunitz, rode down her protests.

There was nothing perfunctory about these. She fought back long and hard. Austria would be discredited for ever. She would not have a friend left in the world. She would be the associate of gangsters and bandits. She would fatally undermine the principles of international morality which she, the Empress, had striven so hard to uphold. She would undergo the worst humiliation rather than share in this crime. But she was ageing now, and Kaunitz and her son manoeuvred her into a position from which there seemed no way out. Her prophecies of woe were indeed fulfilled. Worse by far, by sharing in the first partition of Poland, Austria, though not even Maria Theresa saw this at the time, tied herself to Prussia and Russia. It brought an addition to her territory which made strategic nonsense and injected a new and unassimilable national element. It curtailed her freedom of action. It had a great deal to do with the final ruin of the Empire in years to come.

Joseph's military exploits were absurd to the point of fiasco. Fired by the example of Frederick of Prussia as a great soldier and Catherine of Russia as a successful empire-builder, he was determined that he also would shine and, quite forgetting his dedication to the intellectual enlightenment and the social welfare of his poorer subjects, he led his country into two unhappy wars: the first, again in the teeth of his mother's opposition, was the outcome of what he believed would be a walk-over, the attempt to seize for Austria part of Bavaria after the death of the Elector. To his disgust and dismay his hero Frederick now stepped forward as the peace-maker and upholder of international morality. Undaunted, Joseph put himself at the head of an army of 200,000 and marched into Bohemia to face the Prussians. He was saved from almost inevitable disaster only by the ageing Frederick's firm refusal to be lured into a pitched battle and his mother's activity in concluding an armistice behind his back. Formally this was known as the War of the Bavarian Succession, informally as the 'Potato' War – because Joseph's army, sitting out through a dreary winter in the snow and mud of Bohemia, with nobody to fight, was reduced to living off potatoes dug up with their bayonets in the fields. Again, in 1788, after Maria Theresa's death, Joseph undertook a short and silly war against the Turks, which only added fury to the complaints of a thoroughly disgruntled people. Before he died Hungary and the Netherlands were again in full revolt. It was a sad end to the career of a man who had set out to be the great reforming Emperor. It might, indeed, have been the end of Austria. Joseph died in February 1790. In July the year before the Parisian mob had stormed the Bastille. It was a dangerous moment for the securest throne, let alone a shaky one.

That the throne did not fall was due to Joseph's younger brother, Leopold, Archduke of Tuscany, who became Leopold II. He was forty-three and at the height of his powers. His powers were impressive. It was Austria's double misfortune that this Leopold was born after Joseph and that when he did succeed his brother he had only two years to live. After an unpromising youth he had taken over Tuscany from his father, the Emperor Francis, and turned the Pitti Palace in Florence into the headquarters of the wisest, most equitable, most humane, most progressive (in the true sense of the word, before it was corrupted by doctrinaire ideologies) government on the continent of Europe. He contrived to do this on a shoestring: his little realm was very poor. He had to a remarkable degree some of the finest qualities of his mother, which he infused with the spirit of the day. Far more than his brother he was a true figure of the Enlightenment. Given Joseph's chances, first as co-Regent, then as Emperor, he would have come down to us as Leopold the Wise.

There is a good deal to be said for the monarchical system. Blood, tradition and training applied to the single end of producing rulers do in fact tell. So much so that even a mediocre Habsburg was a specialized professional, more likely to sustain the responsibilities of power over a long lifetime than most other men, even those of far greater ability. The chief defect of the system was that it was never carried to its logical conclusion. Animals bred for a particular purpose are rigorously culled to exclude from the breeding line all individuals with undesirable characteristics. This ruthless system of selection was not applied to the Habsburgs or to any other European dynasty. The nearest thing to a cull was the removal from the scene of the unfortunate

Don Carlos by his father, Philip II of Spain. But such actions were very rare. The remarkable thing is that this extraordinary family managed to produce over the centuries as many able rulers as it did.

Leopold did not have the chance to prove himself constructively. In the two years allotted to him by an extremely inscrutable Providence he was at first highly successful in mending the fences broken by Joseph. He ended the Turkish War, came to terms with the Hungarians and won the confidence of his own Austrian peoples by rescinding almost every edict his brother had ever published. He also, with a mixture of force and conciliatory pledges, made peace with the Netherlands. This was a major achievement in itself; but he made the greatest mistake of his life by giving offence in his conduct of the Netherlands operation to England and Holland. He was determined to put himself under no obligation to the Maritime Powers by invoking their guarantees. He did not see that within a year Austria was going most desperately to need all the help she could get from England.

His error had been to assume that his brother-in-law and formal ally, Louis XVI of France, would soon recover his authority, if in a severely amended form. But as chaos bred chaos in France, as the Girondists breathed fire and destruction on the Emperor for daring to stand up for the rights of the German princes under French suzerainty, the danger of war grew acute. And war between Austria and France meant first and foremost that the Netherlands would immediately be lost. Poor Leopold was caught between the need to avoid war at almost all costs, unless he could call on England's declared support, and the need to rally the crowned heads of Europe to a common front against revolution. England, cool towards Austria because of her recent cold-shouldering in the matter of the Netherlands, declared herself determinedly neutral. Leopold, suspected by the French of actively plotting with Louis, was driven to extreme lengths to show that he was innocent of any intention of intervening in the internal affairs of France – while at the same time devising scheme after scheme, all chimerical, for rescuing Louis and, above all, his own sister, poor Marie-Antoinette, without engaging in war. He was still holding on to the peace when he was take ill with amoebic dysentery and within a matter of days was dead. It was March 1792. Almost immediately France declared war on his successor.

It was during the reigns of Maria Theresa and her two sons that Vienna made its supreme contribution to the musical culture of Europe. Gluck, the son of a forester who had once been gun-bearer to Prince Eugene, owed a great deal directly to the Empress who, although she preferred the Italianate music of her youth, made him her court musician. Neither Haydn nor Mozart, both sons of the people, owed much directly to the court, which found no proper employment for them and never understood their genius. But the society in which they moved and worked owed its existence and stability to the good sense and modesty of Maria Theresa. And it was to the Vienna of Haydn and Mozart that the young Beethoven came from Bonn as the eighteenth century drew to a close, because it seemed to him the best place to learn and to work. So there developed that astonishing line of composers, through Schubert, through Bruckner and the German Brahms, which continued to the last days of the monarchy and beyond, to end in Mahler, Hugo Wolf, Berg, Schoenberg and Webern. There was also the Bohemian-Moravian line. Mozart himself was always happier in Prague than in Vienna, and Prague was kinder to him. Bohemia and Moravia had their own very strong musical cultures, which were to flower under the last great Habsburg in Dvorak, Smetana and the amazing genius, Janáček. It was a long journey from the rococo to atonalism; from the extravagances of Schönbrunn to the architectural revolution of Loos; from Metastasio, the librettist of Gluck, Haydn and Salieri, to Hofmannsthal, the librettist of Richard Strauss. Just as, on another level of human experience, it was a long way from Van Swieten and Joseph II's fine General Hospital to the Vienna Medical School in its heyday – and Dr. Sigmund Freud. But it was a continuous way for more than a century and a half, often rough for the travellers, but safe – until the last great Habsburg, in the summer of 1914, lost his sense of direction and all Europe went off its head.

9

Victory; reaction; collapse:
Francis I, Ferdinand I, and Metternich

THE crying need of Austria as she faced the storms of the revolutionary and Napoleonic wars was for a ruler of genius to rally the Empire and all Europe. This no doubt was asking too much. But she got the next best thing. In Leopold's eldest son, Francis I, the Habsburgs produced yet another born survivor; he stuck it out for forty-three years, from 1792 to 1835, through thick and thin, manoeuvring coolly and quite ruthlessly, accepting major humiliations without turning a hair and the greatest triumphs without exultation. He lived and had his being on a level of understatement which was the perfect foil for the bombast of the times. Thus, for example, after the catastrophe at Austerlitz which drove Austria out of the war, Francis, who was present at the battle, reported to his wife: 'A battle was fought today which did not turn out very well.'

One is reminded of that other great survivor, Frederick III, with his famous saying: 'To forget what cannot be recovered is the supreme felicity.' And, indeed, Francis had something of Frederick's slow metabolism. He made a virtue of it. His gentleness in the family circle, his lethargy, his refusal to fuss, his celebrated lack of pretentiousness, his habitual projection of an amiable, easy-going cynicism, provided not so much a protective shield as a convenient camouflage for one of the toughest and most determined figures in Habsburg history. He would cut his losses with a display of equanimity that at times seemed frivolous. But he knew what he was doing, and why. And he never confused the shadow with the substance. Thus when, in 1806, after the Treaty of Pressburg, the Holy Roman Empire was solemnly abolished under pressure from Napoleon, Francis blandly laid down the Imperial crown, which was never to be worn again. But two years before, seeing the way the wind was blowing, he had given himself a new Imperial style and had himself proclaimed Emperor of Austria, and it was thus as His Imperial and Apostolic Majesty, Emperor of Austria, King of Hungary, that he survived Napoleon's fall and, as the senior monarch, welcomed the majesties and highnesses of Europe to the Congress of Vienna. Again, having quite coldly married his daughter, Marie Louise, to the upstart Emperor who had driven him and all his family out of Vienna and set up house in the palace of Schönbrunn, when Napoleon fell he packed Marie Louise off to be Duchess of Parma but, with the minimum of fuss, sequestered the little Duke of Reichstadt, his grandson, Napoleon's heir, to live out his short life in luxury and terrible frustration within the confines of Schönbrunn.

In the usual view Francis is completely overshadowed by the brilliant figure of his foreign minister, Prince von Metternich. This is inevitable: Metternich had the brains, the diplomatic genius, the vitality and capacity for infinite hard work, the vision. But Metternich needed a firm base from which to operate, and Francis, far from being clay in the hands of his chief minister, provided that firm base. He was happy to give Metternich the credit for everything; Metternich earned it. Further, it was convenient to have, in this professional diplomat from the Rhineland with his unsurpassed vanity and self-satisfaction, a figurehead who could divert from himself the anger of his own subjects at unpopular measures and the frequent indignation of the governments of other powers. If Metternich had not existed, Francis would have invented him – if, inevitably, in a less dazzling form. As things were, he was sent from heaven. He came to dominate Europe, which was just what was required, while Francis could make a great play perambulating the streets of Vienna like any bourgeois, pottering in his hot-houses at Schönbrunn, dropping into the kitchen to make toffee. He actually enjoyed doing these things; but he would have done them, or something like them, in any case. This man who had been bullied by his uncle Joseph in his youth, and then been deeply shaken by the mess that domineering uncle had made of the affairs of the realm, faced then by the revolutionary violence in France and the death of his aunt on the guillotine, was seized with the need for a hand of iron; but he understood that the times called for a velvet glove.

It is also to be remembered that he put his own stamp upon his time and survived early calamity for some years before Metternich took over. He and Austria were at first very much alone and it was Austria in Italy which had to meet and bow to the first terrible onslaught of Napoleon. England was fighting hard at sea, and it was Nelson himself who rescued that other aunt of Francis's, Maria Theresa's spirited daughter Caroline, married to Ferdinand IV of Naples, Emma Hamilton's dearest friend. But on the Continent there was little help for Austria and much embarrassment. Vienna itself was occupied in 1805, the year of Trafalgar, after the Austrian defeat at Ulm. Then came Austerlitz and the break-up of the old Empire, with many German princes running for cover and forming the Confederation of the Rhine. Francis, as already observed, kept his head. It was not until 1809 that Metternich, who had been ambassador to a number of European courts, assumed office in Vienna. This was also the year in which Austria, seeing France in difficulties with Wellington in Spain, decided to fight again and started off in fine style with the defeat of the French by the Emperor's brother, the Archduke Charles, at Aspern, just across the Danube from Vienna and very close to the site of Rudolph I's defeat of the Bohemian king at the battle of the Marchfeld in 1278. Immediately after that Napoleon had his revenge at Wagram. Francis himself watched that battle, in which the slaughter was very great. Napoleon brought 180,000 men against Charles's 130,000. The battle raged for two days, with the Austrians mounting a powerful counter-offensive on the morning of the second day. The French lost 30,000, the Austrians 25,000. As Francis watched the final withdrawal of his brother's forces, with the French too exhausted to pursue, he turned away, impassive as always: 'Now, I think, we'd better go home.'

It was Metternich's first task to buy peace as economically as possible, his second to keep it. The giving in marriage of a Habsburg princess to the man who had started life as a Corsican lieutenant was the main part of the price. Francis calmly paid it. It was unheroic but it was wise. There was no question in his mind of humiliation. Habsburgs were above humiliation. They needed no false pride. Their real pride was devouring and untouchable. So long as the Emperor existed he also was untouchable. He continued to exist.

Metternich's peace did not last long. It was a bizarre interlude in Habsburg history. The Netherlands had gone, Napoleon's family lorded it on what had been Habsburg thrones in Italy and Spain, and Vienna, now a glittering city of balls and waltzes, was filled with Habsburg refugees. The Empire had gone. Many of the German princes had allied themselves with France. Prussia was defeated and savagely humiliated. But Francis, with Metternich at his elbow, still ruled over the Austrian lands (minus certain provinces subtracted by Napoleon), Bohemia, Moravia, Silesia – and Hungary. In 1812 he and his Empress engaged on a state progress to Dresden to attend the dazzling reception which was Napoleon's send-off for his Russian campaign. Four months later Napoleon was back in Dresden, exhausted, haggard and unshaven, on his flight back to Paris from Moscow. And now it was time for Austria to fight again, this time with Russia and Prussia. Leipzig was fought and won. While England fought successfully in Spain, the continental allies closed in on Paris. And Napoleon was forced into the act of abdication in favour of the son, Napoleon II, who was never to reign but was to live and die as the Duke of Reichstadt at Schönbrunn.

It was a miracle, and Francis and Metternich were on hand to celebrate it. The great celebration was the Congress of Vienna at which Francis acted the host, as cool in triumph as he had been in defeat, and Metternich was the organizing genius, moving in a sort of delirium of purposeful activity and multilateral intrigue. His object was to keep emperors and kings amused while he and the visiting ministers re-drew the map of Europe in accordance with his own ideas. On both counts he succeeded, but it took a very long time. The big four were Austria, England, Russia and Prussia, represented at the conference on the Ballhausplatz by Metternich, Castlereagh, Nesselrode and Hardenberg. But Talleyrand, the spokesman of the defeated power, from the outset showed himself to be such a master of intrigue that in self-defence the victors brought him in to all their deliberations; and it was Talleyrand's mission and amusement to delay matters by bringing up an endless succession of procedural points and to sow suspicion and discord among the victors, inside and outside the conference room.

Alexander I of Russia, who saw himself, excusably, as the saviour and arbiter of Europe, with Frederick William III of Prussia headed the list of over two hundred royal and princely families with their various retinues, who all descended on Vienna with an eye to the main chance and a determination to shine and have a splendid time. Behind the princes and the ministers swarmed tens of thousands of private individuals intent on being in the swim or getting what pickings they could: painters, journalists, actors, dancers, pickpockets and whores. From the marvellous Indian summer of 1814 through winter and spring and deep into the summer of 1815, Vienna shone and glittered and danced as never before or since.

Behind the scenes, however, all was far from being plain-sailing. Differences were acute and sometimes bitter. The Congress was frequently on the point of breaking down. For three months on end, for example, Metternich and the Tsar of Russia would not meet. More than once it looked as though the victors were heading straight for war among themselves. The most explosive elements were provided by the erratic ambitions of Alexander of Russia and Frederick William of Prussia at the expense of Poland and Saxony. They were still bickering when, in February 1815, Napoleon landed at Antibes from Elba and started his great march on Paris. Even while the powers girded themselves to destroy him, their representatives in Vienna continued arguing: the final agreements were signed nine days before the battle of Waterloo.

It was to be the last great European carve-up until the reduction of a united Germany and the dismemberment of the Austro-Hungarian Empire just over a hundred years later. There were to be readjustments in the century to come and major shifts in the balance of power, with Austria as the chief loser. But the whole drama of the nineteenth century and the early years of the twentieth, culminating in the 1914 war, was to be played out within the framework established on the eve of Waterloo.

In so far as that framework can be seen as the creation of any one man, the man was Metternich; the only man to approach him in understanding and intelligence was the splendid and maligned Lord Castlereagh. And Metternich sought to set the seal on his 'system' with the Holy Alliance, originally concluded soon after the final abdication of Napoleon, between the Emperors of Austria and Russia and the King of Prussia. Seen first as a declaration of Christian principles on the part of the monarchies of Europe, this alliance became in effect a treaty of mutual insurance, a sort of monarchs' trade union, a defensive barrier against revolution and subversion. Neither Metternich nor Francis regarded it as an instrument of reaction. For the Emperor it was a formal statement of the obvious, a reaffirmation of the *status quo* so rudely interrupted by the French Revolution. To Metternich it appeared in a more constructive light. He had a vision. With all his personal failings, his brilliant and unscrupulous opportunism, he was a truly great statesman. He wanted peace, stability, prosperity. All three were imperilled by rivalry between the powers and the forces of subversion within the individual powers. Austria, of course, must be great. But Austria could be great and prosperous only within the framework of a stable Europe. Past Habsburgs had dreamt of uniting Europe beneath the Imperial crown. When that dream vanished for ever there was nothing to stand in the way of the practice of unbridled power-politics. Thus, for example, Richelieu, with all his gifts, had concerned himself only with the greatness of France: Kaunitz had worked only for the greatness of Austria, sweeping aside with the aid of Joseph II the scruples of Maria Theresa, who was the first monarch to understand the need for an international order based on integrity and the pledged word: Pitt strove for England, seeing the continental powers almost exclusively as elements to be balanced as part of a great design which allowed free play for British interests.

Metternich was the first League of Nations man, born long before his time; the first statesman to perceive Europe as an organic whole which must be induced to prosper as a whole if the parts were to flourish – above all, of course, the part for which he himself was responsible: the Habsburg Empire. When he remarked, 'I should have been born in the year 1900 with the twentieth century before me', he was speaking more truly than anyone believed. To him the Concert of Europe was a real and vivid concept. His tragedy was that Europe was changing out of all recognition even as he spoke. The pattern he sought to impose, or induce, failed completely to allow for the rise of the bourgeoisie, still less for the development of nationalist ideals.

Certainly the Emperor Francis was never to appreciate the Metternich dream, although he fully understood the need for the monarchs to hang together, even if this called for some sacrifice of individual ambition to the common good. He was not a dreamer, neither was he ambitious. As already observed, he was first and foremost a survivor. It was enough for him that his dynasty had in fact survived the Napoleonic storm. The Netherlands had gone for ever, to be absorbed in the new kingdom which was, later still, to be divided into Holland and Belgium. But the Empire had finished up with another slice of Galicia, carved out of the body of Poland, with a small portion of Bavaria, and with lands in Italy and on the Adriatic coast. Even less than Metternich, who was aware of the need for internal reform, did Francis recognize the validity of forces which could not be controlled by the Imperial will. He could appreciate the value of a compact with his fellow monarchs, but the idea of a compact between the monarch and his subjects was alien to him. The Metternich system, domestically, called for a very tight rein on all the subject peoples and rigid central rule backed by an active censorship and a powerful political police force.

This suited Francis down to the ground. He was benevolent. If his subjects obeyed him they could count on paternal protection of a most amiable kind. If they did not, then they were disturbers of the peace, and prison was the place for them. His instincts spoke out most clearly in the celebrated question which he put to one of his entourage who was praising the patriotic fervour of a distinguished servant of the Empire: 'But is he a patriot for me?' Loyalty to the Habsburg crown was the only thing that mattered, a concept he carried so far that when the great Tyrolean patriot, Andreas Hofer, led his mountain countrymen in spontaneous rebellion against the French and the Bavarians, fighting for reunion beneath the Imperial crown, Francis was not pleased He allowed his enemy Napoleon to take Hofer away and shoot him: the last thing he wished to encourage was a popular rising, even a rising in his favour. Thus it was that Metternich's cloudy and intermittent perceptions of the forces of change were damped down and nullified by a Habsburg master who thought he could forbid all change by Imperial decree.

Change, nevertheless, was in the air. In the early nineteenth century we see for the first time the development under a Habsburg of autonomous popular forces, and this, paradoxically, owed much to Metternich, indeed to Francis himself. The Metternich era was far from being the period of stagnation that is generally envisaged. It was stagnant only in the sense that after 1815 Austria fought no wars and undertook no radical internal reforms and suffered beneath the censorship of ideas. But it was a period of very swift economic expansion and outstanding prosperity. The Austrian industrial revolution got under way immediately after the Congress of Vienna. The newly acquired provinces of Lombardy and Venetia, fertile and very rich, were included in the Austrian customs area and at once provided a new market for the industrial provinces of old Austria. The Emperor himself created a court authority for the fostering of commerce, above all for attracting experts and technicians of all kinds from abroad. First came looms from England, then Watt's steam-engine. Behind Metternich's 'Chinese Wall', raised against politically subversive influences from abroad, foreign industrialists proliferated, and nearly all the factories started in the first half of the nineteenth century were build by Englishmen, Frenchmen, Swiss, Belgians and Rhinelanders. It was under Francis and Metternich that the economic unity of the Empire was created on the lines of a regional division of labour.

For a time all went very well. It was not until the first crisis of capitalism in the hungry 'forties, when Francis was dead, that the industrial revolution began to get out of hand. Unemployment began to rise dreadfully. The new factories in the towns were too few to make work for the children of the poor peasants who came swarming in from the mountains and the plains to seek their fortunes, adding their number to the destitute handicraft workers whose traditional way of life was going to pieces under the impact of factory production. By then, however, the radical intelligentsia, springing from the new bourgeoisie, had long been seized with the spirit of revolutionary discontent which was fermenting all over Europe – a spirit which, in Austria, was not destroyed but only driven underground, and thus exacerbated, by the Metternich system. Francis never even began to see that there could be all the difference in the world between the expression of doubt over received ideas, demands for social betterment, for a more open and equitable society under the Imperial crown, and the spirit of violent revolution. He could not see that the new prosperity upon which he prided himself was inseparable from the growth of social consciousness, and that this social consciousness should be the dynamo of the future. He could not see that the life of his Empire, which for so many centuries had been controlled by the Crown, owing its glories to the patronage of the Crown, had gathered a momentum of its own and was fast developing in many ways without the assistance of the Crown, often, indeed, in spite of the Crown.

One example of particular relevance to Austria, largely cut off by the censorship from the free expression and development of contemporary ideas, was music.

Gluck, contemporary with Maria Theresa, had been essentially a court composer, pursuing his revolutionary course in Vienna and Paris under the patronage of monarchs who did not understand what he was doing. Haydn, who lived from 1732 to 1809 and died during Napoleon's occupation of Vienna with a French guard of honour posted at his door, owed his existence to the patronage of a princely Hungarian family, the Esterhazy; even though in his later years he came to London and was fêted by a far more broadly based musical society, and was offered a home at Windsor by George III. Mozart never had a job at court, but he actively sought one and depended largely on princely patronage. Beethoven, who came to Vienna in 1792, found his patronage where he could, sometimes from noble families, sometimes among the bourgeois. He could dedicate the 'Eroica' Symphony to Napoleon and cancel the dedication when his hero made himself Emperor. At the time of the Congress of Vienna he was living his own life, owing nothing to the kings and king-makers, though *Fidelio* was performed for the Congress delegates: he arranged his own concerts, made his own terms with publishers. Schubert from the beginning to the end of his short life lived on a shoestring, patronized intermittently by wealthy music-lovers, but finding his friends among bourgeois amateurs and fellow-musicians. By then the long line of independent theatres had been running for nearly fifty years, increasingly sustaining by private enterprise an artistic tradition which owed less and less to the court.

Francis died in 1835, leaving the throne to his feeble son, Ferdinand, epileptic, mentally arrested, but a man of the sweetest nature in the world. Metternich had worked for this succession because he believed with an imbecile Emperor on the throne he, Metternich, would be in effective control of the Empire and thus able to put through the domestic reforms he himself now saw to be necessary if the intellectual and economic life of the realm was to keep pace with the times. But Francis still had a shot in his locker which went off after he was dead. In his will he appointed a State Council, which included Count Kolowrat, Metternich's most devoted enemy, and the man who had obstinately frustrated all his attempts at internal reform during the reign of Francis. So it was to continue. But within a few years of Ferdinand's accession the underground currents began to gather strength, then to converge, until, in 1848, with revolutionary activity mounting all over Europe, they broke the surface and in a swiftly rising flood all but swept the House of Habsburg into limbo.

The signal for revolt came, once more, from Paris, when, in February 1848, Louis-Philippe was driven from the throne, the monarch replaced by a new republic with the gifted adventurer and intriguer, the nephew of the great Napoleon, Napoleon III, as its president. Soon the German princes were fighting and manoeuvring to preserve their thrones. The King of Prussia was forced to grant a constitution. In Dresden the revolutionary movement against the royal House of Saxony was encouraged by men as disparate as the Russian anarchist Bakunin and the thirty-five-year-old composer Richard Wagner. In England the Chartists were preparing their monster petition which ended in fiasco.

Throughout the Habsburg realm the movement of revolt, which for some years had been prepared by pamphleteers (who were forced to have their products printed outside the Empire, then smuggled in), was complex in the extreme. While the bourgeoisie as a whole, above all in Vienna, took life as it came, making jokes about the secret police but on the whole adopting an air of cynical resignation to the restrictions on political liberty, some members of the intelligentsia, as well as more than a sprinkling of aristocratic members of the provincial diets, even of the army general staff, were expressing open discontent with the system. They wanted to open windows to the fresh air of progress; they wanted freedom of speech; above all they demanded an end to absolutism: the Emperor must grant a constitution. At the same time the very existence of a multi-national state was being threatened by the spirit of nationalism: Lombardy and Venetia for the Italians; Hungary for the Magyars; Bohemia for the Czechs. Nor was this nationalistic wave confined to Slavs, Magyars, Italians and some Poles: the Germans of the old Austrian lands had become self-conscious, thinking in terms of race and revolting against a supra-national monarchy which saw the German Austrians as one subject race among others. And deep down beneath all this articulate discontent there were ugly stirrings, as yet unapprehended, in the lower depths of society, among the workers of the towns, hard hit by the brutal and impersonal workings of the new industrial age.

The revolt broke out in Vienna on 13 March 1848, starting quietly enough with demonstrations by the university students, those same students who only a fortnight earlier had seemed carefree enough when they cheered their heads off for the composer Meyerbeer, for Liszt, for Jenny Lind. There was nothing at all in their demands that could not have been met and fully satisfied by the conceding of some sort of constitution, the right to free speech, the establishment of a 'liberal' parliament, an elementary bill of rights. Everyone knew that Ferdinand was an imbecile, everyone adored him and felt protective towards him. All the ills of the day were blamed on the State Council, Ferdinand's uncle the uninspired Archduke Ludwig, Kolowrat, above all, unfairly, on Metternich. While the students demonstrated in Vienna for these elementary freedoms, to allow the peoples of the Empire to combine freely in their own mutual interest, there were simultaneous demonstrations in Milan, in Venice, in Budapest, in Pressburg, in Prague, in Cracow. With a show of sense and conciliation the State Council in Vienna could have put itself at the head of a strong unifying movement. Instead it started shooting, and, with the fighting that followed on the shooting, the hungry masses issued from the slums and the back-streets, bent on violence for its own sake.

In the Hofburg there was shock and dismay. Metternich was thrown to the wolves and fled into exile in England; wild promises were made. It was too late. From March to December there was chaos. Ferdinand was spirited away from Vienna to Innsbruck, then back again, then once more to Olmütz. Provisional ministers tried to cope with the disorder in the capital, in vain. The whole Empire was in flames, and soon the very existence of the monarchy depended on the will of one person, a woman, Sophie of Bavaria, married to the new Habsburg heir, the Archduke Charles, by no means an imbecile like his brother, but weak and irresolute. Sophie discovered in herself extraordinary reserves of courage and determination. It was she who held things together while the Imperial generals bombarded Prague into submission, then beat the Italians at Custozza, then turned to deal with Hungary, taking a now embattled Vienna by bombardment and storm on the way. Hungary, which had thrown up a national leader of immense power and conviction in the figure of Lajos Kossuth, was clearly going to be a very tough nut to crack. But by the autumn the time had come for the Crown to reassert itself through the rest of the Empire. The problem was, who should wear it?

Sophie, the generals, and a brilliant, incisive, relentless, immensely ambitious scion of one of Austria's oldest families, Prince Felix Schwarzenberg, between them hammered out the answer. Schwarzenberg, designated the new prime minister, was obviously the strong man of the future. He would hold the fort in Vienna while his uncle, Prince Windischgrätz, subdued Bohemia and Hungary and the grand and tough old hero of the Napoleonic wars, Radetzky, held down Italy. Ferdinand must clearly abdicate. But was Charles man enough to take his place? Sophie, his most dutiful wife, who had lived for the day when she would be Empress, decided, reluctantly but quite firmly, that he was not.

Further, it was desirable to entrust the throne to a new Emperor who had had no part in the troubles and bitterness of the past. That Emperor should be her son, Francis Joseph, just eighteen, a youth of great promise, proved courage, a clear, cool head and fine appearance. She Sophie, would be Empress-Mother.

10

Recovery and the long last act: Francis Joseph and Charles I

APART from a short and painful epilogue, meaningless and vain, the rest of the Habsburg story is the story of Francis Joseph. And the story of Francis Joseph was a long stone-walling action, unparalleled in history, against the forces of disintegration, which ended, quite suddenly, in the final collapse not only of the Habsburg Empire but also of the old European order so laboriously built up, so precariously sustained, and the substitution of the world we know today. Vienna was the *Kaiserstadt*, the Imperial city *par excellence*, never more glittering, splendid, proud, than when its very existence was being steadily, inexorably undermined – never more productive, too (this is sometimes forgotten), of the things of the spirit and the mind. Its astonishing efflorescence of outstanding figures, drawn from all corners of the Empire, on the very edge of the *debâcle*, laid down a great part of the intellectual capital on which the world has been living since the First World War. It is useful to remember that Sigmund Freud, who came to Vienna from Moravia, did his stint as an army doctor in the service of the Emperor – and enjoyed it.

Over this city, this doomed empire, Francis Joseph reigned for sixty-eight years, transformed by time and by his own will from the brash and arrogant young autocrat of eighteen into a venerated father-figure: more than this, he came to be seen as a living sacrifice, a scapegoat, bowed down by the weight of his public and personal disasters and, at the same time, bearing on his slight shoulders the burden of the sins of all his subjects. At the end he was quite alone: his brother Maximilian, Emperor of Mexico, had been shot by a revolutionary firing squad and his sister-in-law driven mad; his son, the Crown Prince, had killed himself at

Mayerling; his Empress, adored but long estranged from him, had been stabbed to death on the quayside at Geneva; Francis Ferdinand, his nephew, his new heir, had married beneath his station, opposed him in every way, and had died at Sarajevo with his morganatic wife by the assassin's bullet which precipitated the 1914 war; even his faithful friend and mistress, Katherina Schratt, his only confidante, had deserted him long before.

In the palaces and ballrooms of the capital the life of high society, all focused on the court, continued with unabated extravagance and brilliance. But the master of the court, the ageing Emperor, ruling through professional bureaucrats and politicians, was withdrawn from that life, emerging only for specific functions of state, or to inspect his beloved army, or to attend an archducal wedding. He toiled by day, endlessly, unrelentingly, over the paper reflections of everything that took place in his vast dominions, slept briefly by night on his narrow bed in the Hofburg, or in Maria Theresa's immense rococo palace at Schönbrunn, for all the world as though should he deviate by a hairsbreadth from routine, the great and lovely city, the whole Empire, would fly to pieces. He died in 1916, in the middle of the terrible war into which, too old and weary to resist any more, he had allowed bad advisers to drag him. He was eighty-six. Within two years of his death the Empire indeed flew to pieces.

'Farewell my youth!' he had murmured when summoned to the ceremony in the ancient fortress of Olmütz which put him at the head of an empire of forty million souls, some still fighting for their independence, others beaten, crushed and bitterly resentful. He had been, until the past year, a pleasant, gay, warm-hearted boy – handsome in a narrow-faced way, slight but very well built, highly presentable, a good dancer, intelligent without being clever, open to experience without being imaginative, very good at drawing – and, as some of his drawings show, with a natural sense of humour. He was in love with uniforms and ceremonial drill – a perfectly valid, if limited, expression of the aesthetic impulse: a fact not widely understood – as well as with joy in power. He had survived his baptism of fire with Radetzky in Italy and been steady under it. Now, under Schwarzenberg, he had to put himself to school. Schwarzenberg, brilliant, almost recklessly arrogant and dismissive, contemptuous of ordinary mortals, believed in putting the people in their place. At the same time he despised his fellow aristocrats who had allowed the monarchy to drift to the verge of destruction. By all means let there be a parliament; but who was fit to run one? The masses must be led and commanded; the liberals among the bourgeoisie and lesser nobility were windbags; the nobility had failed in their duty. So even while the new politicians were working out a constitution, Schwarzenberg was preparing to strangle it at birth. He found an eager pupil in the young Emperor who saw himself, a Habsburg, as God-chosen, who put his trust in his great army, a coming together under one flag of all the nationalities, to form a multi-racial state within the state, loyal not to the peoples but to him alone.

In this mood Francis Joseph steeled himself to be a tyrant. Since he knew next to nothing about his peoples this was all the easier. He stood by, lending all his authority to Schwarzenberg, while this strange and difficult man restored the Empire, organized it on autocratic lines, defied the opinion of the outside world, revolted by his Draconian measures, and made it appear stronger than it had ever been before: so strong that he was able to go out of his way to reassert Austrian dominance in central Europe, humiliating Prussia. Schwarzenberg had only four years to live before he died prematurely in 1852. It was during these four years that the white tunics of the Imperial army came to stand in the eyes of liberal opinion everywhere as a symbol of hardness and oppression. In the greater part of an Empire that army simply stood guard over peoples now cowed and sullen. But in Hungary the revolution developed under the leadership of Kossuth into a full-scale war of liberation, so bitterly fought that the young Emperor, invoking the Holy Alliance, called the Tsar of Russia to his aid. Nicholas was only too ready to give that aid, to assist in the repression of rebellion, to gain influence and put Austria under an obligation. He sent in a powerful army, and it was to a Russian general, not to Austria, that the Hungarians at last surrendered. There were some in Vienna who saw future danger in this development. Their fears were justified. But Schwarzenberg was unperturbed. 'Austria,' he is said to have remarked 'will astonish the world with her ingratitude!' Certainly, she astonished the Tsar, and outraged him too.

With the defeat of the Hungarian revolt the monarchy was again supreme. Francis Joseph, the loneliest of figures now, coped with his own youthful inadequacy and vulnerability by armouring himself against human feeling. He had allowed Radetsky to punish the Italians. Now he watched while Schwarzenberg savagely condemned the Hungarian rebels, some of them of ancient families, to death or long imprisonment. Peace was restored, but it was the peace of the graveyard. A young Emperor, chosen to make a new start, introduced in the middle of the nineteenth century an absolutist regime more rigid and harsh than any Habsburg had attempted since the Thirty Years' War. The Habsburg possessions, now as never before in history, were subjected to an unbending central tyranny based on and managed by an impersonal bureaucracy, efficient, incorruptible, but loathed. Now, and for nearly two decades to come, the Hungarians themselves lost their special position upheld through so many reigns.

It could not last. Francis Joseph was driving his peoples too hard. He was also driving himself too hard. He worked as few monarchs had ever worked before. With Schwarzenberg dead, he depended too much on inferior advisers – technicians for domestic affairs like Alexander Bach, technicians for foreign affairs like Count Buol-Schauenstein, technicians for military affairs like Count Grünne. They were none of them up to the job. Francis Joseph in his early twenties lacked even a shadow of the profound instinct which told his great ancestor, Maria Theresa, also in her early twenties, whom to listen to, whom to ignore, and, miraculously, how and where to find good men. Between them, from 1852 onwards, Francis Joseph and his ministers were driving straight towards catastrophe.

And Francis Joseph, alone, was driving towards catastrophe in his private life. He might appear to the outer world to be arrogant, cold, unbending: he was determined so to appear. But he could still fall in love. In 1853 he brought the first gleam of warmth and hope to a dead and sullen Vienna by presenting as his bride a ravishing beauty, an enchantress, tender, romantic and afraid, his cousin Elisabeth of Bavaria.

Elisabeth's tragedy, the Emperor's too, is one of the best-known stories of modern times. She was crushed by the rigidities of court protocol, she was bullied and nagged at by a formidable mother-in-law, determined to make this gay, wild, rather silly creature with her passion for poetry and horses into a proper figure of an Empress, she was alienated by her husband's obsession with work and his deference towards his mother. Driven away from her husband and into herself, she escaped into a fantasy world which soon expressed itself in physical flight, so that she spent a lifetime on the wing – she flew from her husband and her duties; she flew from herself and her own self-admitted failure, always travelling, like a bird driven by the winds, riding, riding, ever more recklessly as though seeking to break her own neck, making her own beauty, her incomparable figure, into something like a cult, and ever and again she would come briefly to rest to be with her husband, usually in a moment of crisis, to show the world what a magnificent Empress she could have been, to stand by him after a lost battle, even to arrange and lend her protection to his sole truly human relationship, his friendship with the actress Katherina Schratt, to break the news of the suicide of Rudolph, her only son.

For many years, such was the Emperor's outward image, the world believed that Francis Joseph alone was to blame for her unhappiness: she was passionate and warm; he was cold and re-pellent. When, after the monarchy had fallen, their letters were found and published, it was seen that the story was quite other-wise. This man, so remote and forbidding, was, for forty-five years until her death in 1898 on that far quayside in Geneva, on his knees to a passionately adored and cruel goddess, 'my dearest angel Sisi', whom he could never capture. And of course this calamity did nothing but steel him to hide his wounded spirit behind a front of iron.

The marriage began to go wrong from the very start. Sophie, who should have striven to bring the young girl out, was largely responsible: she commanded. Francis Joseph himself was largely responsible: immature and inexperienced, weighed down by his own immense responsibilities, he could not see that Elisabeth was so much more immature and inexperienced. As time went on Elisabeth herself became responsible; but, unlike her equally beautiful sister, married to the gross King of Naples, she never grew up. Refusing to make the best of a bad job, but enjoying the privileges of her supreme position, she never forgave. The Emperor, shattered in his deepest feelings, was thus emotionally starved for the remainder of his life. For some years, indeed, he was emotionally crippled. It took a major personal defeat to shock him into an awareness of the realities involved in the running of an empire.

The shock was the battle of Solferino in 1859 and the consequent loss of his cherished and rich Italian possessions.

The same combination of uncertainty, fear of the unknown, and trust in military might that had led the young Emperor to isolate himself from his peoples soon after Schwarzenberg's death led him also to isolate Austria from the rest of Europe. It was as though he could only prove himself as a ruler by keeping his fellow rulers at arm's length. And the first fruits of this aloofness, this almost hysterical rejection of anything that looked like patronage from monarchs and foreign statesmen with three times his years and experience, was the attitude adopted by Austria towards the antagonists in the Crimean War.

When Nicholas I, assuming the role of the great protector of all Christians still living under Turkish rule, moved his army into Moldavia after the other powers had refused to join him in carving up what remained of the enfeebled Ottoman Empire, 'the sick man of Europe', Palmerston's England and France under Napoleon III were determined to stop him. Austria found herself between two fires. She owed a debt of gratitude to Russia who now counted on her support. On the other hand, the idea of powerful Russian influence in the Balkans appealed to Francis Joseph no more than the idea of Russian penetration to the Mediterranean appealed to France and England. But by keeping Austria out of the war he ended up by getting the worst of both worlds. At the end of the Crimean War, at the Peace of Paris in 1856, Austria found herself cold-shouldered by both the British and the French – although she had in fact tied up a large Russian army on the Galician frontier – and an object of hatred on the part of Russia. It was the mood engendered by the Peace of Paris that was to make her especially vulnerable to the first major assault on the Empire three years later.

Francis Joseph had the misfortune not only to live in an age of change and ferment notable for the rise of nationalism on the part of the weak and of empire-building and jingoism on the part of the strong, but also to be opposed by two of the most gifted statesmen the world has ever seen, Bismarck and Cavour. He, Francis Joseph, was *par excellence* the upholder of the *status quo* in Europe. He had nothing to gain by change. He had everything to lose. He was the heir to the ages. In his veins, through his great-grandfather Leopold II, ran the blood of Maria Theresa; through her the blood of the first Rudolph; of Frederick III, the great survivor; of Maximilian I, the last of the knights and the master of Burgundy; of Charles V, the magnificent, who came so near to reviving and expanding Charlemagne's imperial dream; of Ferdinand II with his holy war against the heretics; of Leopold I whose generals had shattered the menace of the Turks and the glory of Louis XIV; of the whole long line of Habsburgs, of most of the great ruling Catholic families as well. His grandfather Francis had survived Napoleon and presided over the Vienna Congress at which Metternich had sought to achieve a European balance designed to last for ever. It was the new young Emperor's task, unquestioned, God-given, to keep things as they were, to cling to his inheritance and hand it down intact, coping with the manifold internal difficulties as they arose, manoeuvring and later, when at last he comprehended the necessity, to accommodate his rule to the spirit of the age.

In all Europe, however, he was alone in his attachment to the *status quo*. Russia, the unknown giant, was stirring, threatening the equilibrium of the Balkans, reaching out to Constantinople and the Straits. The young Bismarck in Prussia, far-seeing, infinitely subtle, without a scruple in the world, was developing the dream which would drive him to push Austria out of Germany and unite all its parts under the Prussian king, his master. In Paris, the adventurer Napoleon III was possessed with dreams of glory.

Much nearer home, in Turin, a lawyer of genius, Count Cavour, first minister to the Sardinian king, Victor Emmanuel, was scheming brilliantly and with marvellous tact and discretion to turn the uprush of nationalist feeling among the Italians to his master's advantage by uniting all Italy under the Sardinian crown: exploiting the popular appeal of the rebel heroes, Mazzini and Garibaldi, for his own ends.

Cavour's first step was to get Austria out of Lombardy, a hopeless task for tiny Piedmont without an extremely powerful ally: the whole weight of the Imperial army, based on the impregnable Quadrilateral south of Lake Garda – the great fortresses of Peschiera, Mantua, Legnano and Verona – could be brought to bear on any force advancing from Turin. Cavour found his ally in Napoleon III, eager for military renown, bent on appearing as the chivalrous champion of the oppressed, greedy for the chance to win Nice and Savoy for France. His next task was to provoke Austria into declaring war: there was no future for Cavour as an open aggressor. This was difficult; it should have been impossible. But to Cavour's patient cunning was allied the clumsy, shortsighted arrogance of Francis Joseph's foreign minister, Buol-Schauenstein, who, reacting to incessant goading like an angry bull, charged blindly into the trap in spite of the frantic efforts of others, above all the English, to restrain him. The result, for Francis Joseph, was total disaster. His beloved army, incompetently led, inadequately provisioned, instead of overwhelming the Piedmontese before the French could arrive in strength, waited on the defensive to be beaten at Magenta by the French and the Piedmontese and driven back past Milan. Francis Joseph himself, shocked and appalled, hurried down from Vienna to take personal command. On the hillside at Solferino above the Mincio river two Emperors faced each other at the head of two vast armies which neither knew how to command. Blundering into each other in the morning mist the two armies met head-on in one of the most terrible battles of the nineteenth century. In the end the Austrians broke, retreating from the field on which lay nearly 40,000 dead.

That night Francis Joseph, still only twenty-nine, outwardly calm but inwardly shattered, wrote to Elisabeth: 'I know what it is like to be a beaten general.'

This was the first great blow. He had lost Lombardy for ever. He had also lost all confidence in his advisers and most of his generals. And he knew he had been inhabiting a fool's paradise. No Habsburg had ever cried aloud over spilt milk. Francis Joseph knew how to cut his losses with the best of his forebears. But he must also set to work to reorganize his realm. He had new ministers now. He demanded to be told the worst about the popular mood and the state of the army and the economy. He was told much that was bad.

And so he embarked, in 1859, on the long process by which he sought to accommodate the most ancient dynasty in Europe to the nineteenth century. He still had a great deal to learn. It was evident, though it called for a revolution in his thinking, that he could no longer act without regard to popular feeling. There had to be an approach to constitutionalism, or at least the appearance of it. But though there might be, must be indeed, open political debate, the last word was still to be with him, the Emperor. This meant, in practice, that the first phase of parliamentarianism in Austria was a charade. Indeed, Francis Joseph saw it as such: 'Now we are going to have a little parliamentarianism', he wrote to his mother in 1861, 'but all power stays in my hands, and the general effect will suit Austrian circumstances very well indeed.'

What started as a charade was soon to develop into an Emperor's education. He tried out a succession of ministers. He rang the changes on representatives of a variety of interests – the dominant polarization was between those German liberals who believed in bureaucratic centralism and the conservative nobility of the various lands who sought to win ascendancy by strengthening the powers of the provincial diets. And in so doing Francis Joseph gave himself a first-class object lesson in the intractable realities of his multi-national Empire, in the strains and stresses produced by nationalist aspirations and class antagonisms, in the problems that might be solved by the exercise of tact and patience (and the individuals who might help to solve them) and the problems there could be no hope of solving. During the eighteen-sixties, in a word, the Emperor, still in his thirties, was transformed from an ignorant, unreflecting autocrat into an expert on the complex affairs of his realm. But he had to suffer yet another blow of the first magnitude, more damaging even than the loss of Italy, before he had learnt his lesson and come to understand that his future duty as supreme ruler lay in finding ways and means of harnessing himself to the needs of his peoples, of serving them, according to his lights, instead of exploiting them for the glory of his House.

The blow came from Prussia, the old enemy, whose king, William I, nevertheless felt a quasi-mystical loyalty to Francis Joseph as heir to the dead Empire and the senior German prince. His new prime minister, Count (later Prince) Otto von Bismarck-Schönhausen, had no such inhibitions. Bismarck's self-appointed task was to make Prussia great and win for her the leadership of a united Germany. He had no desire to destroy Austria. A strong Austria, indeed, was needed as an essential part of the new European balance he envisaged; but she had to be pushed out of Germany and made to understand that her destiny lay elsewhere – towards the East. Even before he assumed office in 1862, this extraordinary genius who embodied in the frame of a giant the brain of a Machiavelli, the will of a Napoleon, the subtlety of the serpent – and, with all this, a neurotic sensibility which would prostrate him in the supreme crises of his life – had formally announced to the British Prime Minister Disraeli: 'As soon as the army shall have been brought to such a condition as to inspire respect, I shall seize the best pretext to declare war on Austria, dissolve the German Diet, subdue the minor states, and give national unity to Germany under Prussia's leadership.' Just so, Habsburg monarchs had dreamed before him. . . .

By 1866 Bismarck was ready. He had not merely to seize the pretext, but to invent it. Like Cavour only seven years earlier, he needed all his skill to manoeuvre Austria into war. But he was more formidable than Cavour, and it would have needed a genius of his quality on the Austrian side to escape the net he spread. He was also lucky. In von Moltke, a regular officer recalled from early retirement, a remarkable combination of scholar, strategist and soldier, he found another genius ready to hand. The outcome was the first *Blitzkrieg*. Prussia marched on 16 June, 1866. By 2 July converging Prussian armies had so pushed the Austrians off balance that their only hope was a strategic withdrawal across the Elbe. But it was too late even for that, and throughout a cold, drenching, unseasonable summer night the Austrians under the veteran Benedek, the only commander who had stood his ground at Solferino, deployed their own forces for a pitched battle, which raged all next day, ending up in the woods around the village of Königgrätz (Sadowa). There were 221,000 Prussians with 776 guns against 214,000 Austrians and Saxons with 770 guns. Both sides fought with unsurpassed, with sacrificial bravery. One Prussian regiment went into battle with 30 officers and 9000 men. It emerged after hand-to-hand fighting with only two officers and 400 men. The last Austrian reserve corps advanced in close formation with flags flying, drums beating, to the tune of a regimental march. In just twenty minutes it lost 279 officers and 10,000 men. The day was above all decided by the superiority of the Prussian needle-gun, the new breech-loading, quick-firing rifle, used for the first time in a major war.

Austria was out of Germany. Four years later Bismarck went on to consolidate Prussian supremacy in Europe as well as in Germany by seizing his chance to fight France, triumphing again through Moltke at Sedan, bringing down Napoleon III, crowning his master as Emperor of the new, unified German Reich at Versailles and, against his better judgement, seizing Alsace and Lorraine ... With what results.

The Habsburgs were out of Germany from which, nearly six hundred years before, they had sprung. Francis Joseph, still only forty years old, took this supreme humiliation with the outward calm and imperturbability which for so long had been the most striking feature of his line. It was humiliation all the more bitter because, in the course of the short war with Prussia, one of his generals, a cousin, the Archduke Albrecht, had soundly beaten Prussia's new ally, Victor Emmanuel, king of the new united Italy, and seemed to be winning Lombardy back for Austria. Now all was gone.

Francis Joseph did not repine. There was pressing need for

action at home. Already before the Prussian onslaught the Hungarians, encouraged by Bismarck, had emerged from their sullen acceptance of submission and put forward bold demands. Francis Joseph, who had firmly set his face against concessions, now saw that he must yield. If he was to hold what remained of his inheritance together he could no longer ignore Hungarian demands for some sort of autonomy. He must find a way, as Maria Theresa had done before him, of winning the Hungarians to his side. He was helped in this by the remarkable character of Hungary's elder statesman, a man of wisdom and moderation, Ferenc Deak, who alone could restrain his fellow-countrymen from violent action, and who was also the first man Francis Joseph had ever met who knew how to talk to him like a father. Drastic in victory, Francis Joseph knew also how to be drastic in defeat. Very well, there would be no half-measures; the whole structure of the monarchy would be transformed. By the great Hungarian Compromise agreement of 1867 the Hungarians should have their own parliament, their own prime minister, responsible directly to Francis Joseph as King of Hungary. The Habsburg Empire was from now on the Dual Monarchy of Austria-Hungary, sharing the person of the Emperor, the army, a joint minister for foreign affairs, and certain financial offices in common. To this new arrangement, which was the final negation of the dream of a centralized Empire, Francis Joseph stuck until the end, with all the stubbornness and tenacity with which he had hitherto upheld the centralized state created for him by Schwarzenberg nearly twenty years earlier. He kept his side of the bargain more loyally than the Hungarians kept theirs. And the working out of the bargain, its consequences in the remainder of the Empire and in the Hungarian lands themselves, was the domestic history of the monarchy for the next half a century.

In essence, Francis Joseph knew that he could not bow to Magyar nationalism without making concessions in the Austrian half of the Empire to Germans, Czechs, Slovenes and Poles. The granting of such concessions, the fluctuating balances of national and racial interest, the bitterness between German and Slav, between Magyar and Slav, the mutual jealousies between different members of the Slav family, later between racialist, anti-Semitic

Germans and liberal idealistic Germans, was to lead to the ultimate paralysis of the new Parliament which had only been set up in 1861. It is fair to say that all the peoples looked to the Crown to protect them from each other and the outside world; but none was prepared to accept the logic of this situation and sacrifice any part of its privileges or its aspirations to the common good. After 1867, the Emperor put aside for ever his concept of himself as an autocrat. His task now was to hold the ring. It was to keep the outside enemy at bay and, through a long succession of ministers of various personalities and political complexions, to nurture the development and self-realization of his subject peoples within the framework of the State. The framework was to be sustained by the Imperial and Royal Army, seen now no longer as the Emperor's personal instrument but, rather, as the one institution in which all the nationalities could come together and evolve a supranational mystique.

But the Germans were not interested in equality with Czechs and Slovenes; the Magyars tyrannized over their own Slavs in Croatia and Dalmatia. Further, dishonouring their compact with the Emperor, their king, they came in time to demand their own national army. All this meant, in practice, that Francis Joseph, as he aged, was ruling as never before. Somebody had to rule. If Czechs and Germans could not sit in the same parliament without coming to blows, the government still had to go on.

It was during this tumultuous period that Vienna finally emerged as the most brilliant city in Europe. The old fortifications containing the ancient inner city were demolished and in their place a vast tree-lined circular boulevard, the *Ringstrasse,* was laid out as the setting for a composition of imposing buildings fit for an Imperial capital at the summit of its glory. To the opera house, already started in 1861, were added in the following decades the new *Burgtheater,* the new University, the Parliament building, the Town Hall, the Palace of Justice, the twin museums of art and natural history, enchanting parks and gardens; the stock exchange too ... Opposite the new art gallery which housed the collections of earlier Habsburgs (above all of Ferdinand I and poor mad Rudolph II) the Hofburg itself, hitherto modest and unassuming, a

hotch-potch of the ages, was given a formidable new wing, surmounted by Imperial eagles, housing majestic state apartments,
and overlooking a vast parade ground, the *Heldenplatz*. Here
equestrian statues of the Archduke Charles, the victor of Aspern,
and Prince Eugene of Savoy, gazed out over the *Ringstrasse* to the
immense monument to Maria Theresa surrounded by her generals
between the two museums. The whole composition might have
been raised to celebrate the foundation of the Empire, which in
fact had just thirty years to go when the statue of the great
Empress was unveiled in 1888.

The beginning of the end was near. It was in January of the
following year that the Crown Prince, the Archduke Rudolph,
thirty-one years old, shot himself, after killing his mistress, Maria
Vetsera, in his hunting-lodge at Mayerling.

The notorious hardness of Francis Joseph, this so complex ruler,
unimaginative yet sensitive to a fault, had manifested itself in in-
defensible actions on a number of occasions since, at nineteen, he
had allowed Schwarzenberg to execute the Hungarian rebel
leaders. It had shown itself when, after Solferino, he had driven
his finance-minister, Bruck, one of the ablest men ever to enter his
service, to suicide by believing an unjust charge against him. It
had shown itself in his treatment of harsh exclusion from the succession of his brother, Maximilian, who had foolishly accepted the
invitation to be Emperor of Mexico which had led to his death by
the hand of a rebel firing squad. It had shown itself when, after the
catastrophe at Sadowa, he had allowed his splendid old rough-
diamond of a general, Benedek, to be broken and made a scapegoat for the mistakes of others, including himself. It had shown
itself in his alienation from his only son, whose liberal dreams he
would not tolerate. It now came out convulsively, and with an
extremity of ugliness, in his attempt to bury the scandal of Rudolph's death. It was to come out once more, very soon, in his
attitude towards his new heir, his nephew Francis Ferdinand of
Este, whom he disliked intensely; above all, in the way he turned
his face against the Archduke's marriage to the Countess Sophie
Chotek, because her very good lineage was yet not good enough to
qualify as a Habsburg bride. When Francis Ferdinand, who was as

stubborn as the Emperor, insisted on marriage he was forced to agree to the exclusion of Sophie's children from the succession. He was not forgiven.

Here, indeed, is a key to the character of the last great Habsburg. The world saw this harshness. It saw little else, because Francis Joseph in his dealings with the world maintained a front of extreme formality and reserve. But to those around him, his ministers, his advisers, he was flexible and genial. His ministers came from all classes and all nationalities. They were all one to him. He could joke with them, humour them, flatter them even. It did not matter: they were not Habsburgs. He could temporize with his subjects: he could give ground to them, and did. But where he would never give way was in any matter affecting the family honour, the name of Habsburg-Lorraine. The weight of his ancestry fell heavily upon his shoulders. The more closely he approached to democratic forms of government the more rigidly and tenaciously he insisted on the integrity of the dynastic idea. All the world was changing: very well, change there must be, and he, the Emperor, as head of State, would countenance it, guide it, encourage it even, according to his lights. But one thing did not, could not change: the House of Habsburg was immutable. It stood apart. And as head of that House it was his duty to sustain it and by every means to emphasize its apartness. Thus it was that an Emperor who was amiability itself in his relations with men of every class ruled his own family, as he ruled himself, with unbending severity. Thus, the families into which a Habsburg could marry were exactly defined. It was not a matter of blood; it was a matter of drawing a line. Cross that arbitrary line and Habsburg became any other family, which was unthinkable: for how could it then pretend to be set apart by God? How could it then pretend to rule?

The ageing Francis Joseph, wise in his perceptions, human and angry in his rejection of what he perceived, knew in his heart that it could not so pretend. The rot had set in. He had seen his brother go prancing off to be a make-believe emperor in a barbarian land. His son Rudolph had killed himself and disgraced his name. His nephew, the Archduke Francis Salvator, had renounced his titles and run away to sea. His new heir put a Countess Chotek above the dynasty. He, the Emperor himself, could not control his own wife and had not the heart to forbid her. More significantly still, the Empire was at last beginning to throw up politicians of integrity, ability and worth – few still, but enough to mark the beginning of a new era – who, given the chance, could show themselves capable of running the State machine as well as any Habsburg. The end was indeed very near, and Francis Joseph sensed it – not of the Empire, not of the multi-national state, not even of the monarchy as such, but of the sort of personal rule which had sustained and been sustained by the members of his family for just over six hundred years. What must come would come. Meanwhile he must continue in the only way he knew.

It did not look like that from the outside. The Empire of Austria-Hungary, the creation of the Compromise of 1867, put on a very good show. It survived the economic crisis of 1873, which coincided with the brilliant World Exhibition in the Prater in Vienna designed to show the world the splendours of Austrian industry and art. It recovered quickly from humiliation at the hands of Prussia and in no time at all was conducting itself very much as a great power in the opening stages of the fearful and hypnotic ritual of bluff and counter-bluff, threat and counter-threat, lie and counter-lie, which was to draw the powers more dangerously together, bristling with arms, in ever-narrowing circles, with ever less room for circumspect manoeuvre, until, in the late summer of 1914, they clashed – and crashed.

The turning point in the international process which was to embroil the powers in the 1914 war was the Franco-Prussian War of 1870 and the subsequent creation of the united German Reich. This finally put an end to any Austrian hope of a return match with Prussia. Henceforward the two central powers, old Austria, new Germany, were to be bound ever more closely together. But the German seizure of Alsace-Lorraine ensured the enduring hostility of France, while renewed Russian activity in the direction of Turkey and the Balkans made inevitable a conflict of interest between St. Petersburg and an Austria excluded from Germany and increasingly looking towards the East.

There was a new and complicating factor: the virtual break-down of the Ottoman Empire in Europe, the rise of an independent Serbia and a quasi-independent Bulgaria, and the revolt of the Serbs and Croats against the Turks in the wild mountain provinces of Bosnia-Herzegovina, which led to the Austrian occupation of those lands in 1878 by agreement with the Powers. The main crisis was the outcome of Russia's victory in the Russo-Turkish war, ending in the Treaty of San Stefano, which placed Russia in a commanding position in the Balkans and brought her to the very gates of Constantinople. This new development threw Europe into confusion and was averted only by the action of Disraeli and Bismarck in organizing the Congress of Berlin, to force a revision of the San Stefano treaty at the cost of great bitterness, and also by the restraining influence exercised by Francis Joseph in Vienna on his own foreign minister (now the Hungarian, Julius Andrassy, whom he had condemned to death in 1849 and then reprieved). But although war was averted, the stage was set for further crises. The Balkans were now wide open to Russian influence and intrigue, so that in due course Serbia, tiny and backward as she was, became in Austrian eyes a standing nightmare, a point of attraction to her own southern Slavs, above all a menace to the Austrian position in Bosnia-Herzegovina.

All went reasonably well so long as Bismarck was in power. This extraordinary figure, who had made his country great by the deliberate and ruthless use of force, was now the apostle of stability and peace. By weaving an intricate network of alliances and agreements, open and secret, he thought, as Metternich had thought before him, that he had achieved a lasting balance. Having concluded a triple alliance with Austria and Italy, his masterstroke was to conclude with Russia the famous Re-insurance Treaty promising Germany neutrality towards Russia unless Russia attacked Austria-Hungary and Russian neutrality towards Germany unless Germany attacked France. All went reasonably well, too, so long as Francis Joseph, also intent on peace, retained complete possession of his powers.

But in 1890 the unimaginable happened. Bismarck was summarily dismissed by his new master, William II, brash, impatient, melodramatic, whose first act of policy was to denounce the

Russian Treaty, throwing Russia into the arms of France. Austria and William's dynamic, mischief-making Germany were now caught between a resentful and restless Russia and a vengeful France – a France, moreover, which was soon to achieve an understanding with England, waking from her self-imposed isolation to face the new facts of the European balance.

There was nobody in Austria to see clearly the unfolding of the massive and terrible movements of the time: in all Europe there were very few who saw. It was the age of material brilliance based on sweated workers who were beginning, ominously, to make their voices heard. It was the age of vulgar display. The dynastic pattern of Europe was settled for ever, it seemed. Major continental war was out of the question. England, France, Germany, the new Belgium too, were carving up Africa among themselves. Russia was turned towards Asia. But if the great dynasties could no longer fight each other, there was a new competition, the competition for prestige. And in their striving to assert themselves the various governments were urged on by the nationalistic ardour of their own peoples, expressed in the headlines and the leading articles of the people's tribunes, the newspapers of the day:

We don't want to fight, but by jingo if we do,
We've got the ships, we've got the men, we've got the money too!

Bismarck had gone, and Francis Joseph, bowed down by his personal tragedies, his public defeats, was getting old. He had lost the unseen fire which for so long he had brought to the management of his ministers. Stubbornly he kept his heir, Francis Ferdinand, at arm's length – and watched him building up what amounted to a shadow opposition government in Prince Eugene's splendid palace, the Belvedere. Francis Ferdinand, rough, angry, frustrated, but honest and bringing a fresh brain to bear on the internal problems of the Empire, should have been used. But the Emperor did not want a fresh brain, least of all his detested nephew's. He would keep things running as they were. He must stick to Germany, much as he distrusted the insufferable young Emperor; he must stick by his Hungarian Compromise, even though the Hungarians, never satisfied, were pressing on him intolerably. Nothing else mattered. He and he alone could keep his peoples from breaking out. But he could no longer lift his eyes to a far horizon. He was unable to check the increasing obsession of his ministers and generals with the awkward, tiny country on the Empire's eastern flank, Serbia, now wide open to Russian intrigue (for after the Russian defeat by Japan in 1904, St. Petersburg had turned once more to the Balkans). He made no effort to restrain Germany in her provocations, above all in her patently obvious attempt to outbuild the British fleet. He permitted the annexation of Bosnia-Herzegovina in 1908, a barren triumph and a fatal one. And when, in June 1914, Francis Ferdinand and his wife were killed by the Bosnian student Gavrilo Princip, evidently with the connivance of Serbia (though this was not proven at the time), he agreed to the despatch of the punitive ultimatum and then, hardly knowing what he was doing, signed the declaration of war which set off the vast, unwilled mobilizations of Russia, then Germany as Austria's ally, then France as Russia's ally, which, once they were ponderously under way, nobody knew how to stop. It was as though he had the death wish on him. Perhaps he had. He was eighty-four years old.

And so, at last, the long history of this most amazing family came to its end because the last powerful ruler of a line long accustomed to viewing the whole map of Europe from a great height was too old and weary in the end to lift his eyes from ridiculous, if irritating, happenings in his own backyard. Francis Joseph died two years later, and his funeral procession was the funeral procession not only of the House of Habsburg, but also of the traditional European order. His heir, his beloved grand-nephew the Archduke Charles, did his best. The war was going well for Austria when the old man died. But it was a ruinous affair, and soon Charles was actively striving to put a stop to it, to disengage his inheritance before it was too late. He failed. After four years of bitter and sacrificial fighting and extreme civilian suffering the fight was lost. Until almost the end the greater part of that Imperial and Royal Army, made up of so many aspiring peoples who had for so long done their best to make the monarchy unworkable, remained, astonishingly, loyal. Now, in defeat, they finally fell apart. The last Habsburg, Charles, stepped down from his throne in November 1918, fully 642 years since the first Rudolph had set up his standard in Vienna. The peoples were set free, all too soon to be swallowed up by the new successors to the Habsburgs, tyrants more cruel and absolute than the old Europe had ever known.

Genealogical Tables

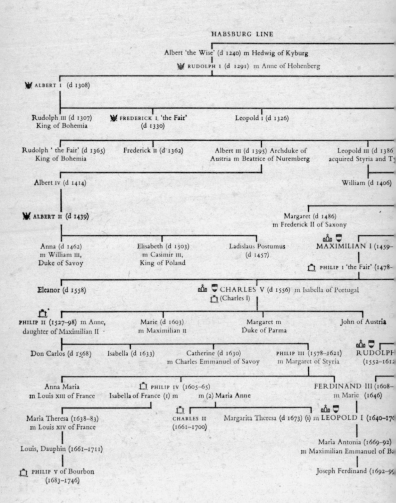

HABSBURG LINE

Albert 'the Wise' (d 1240) m Hedwig of Kyburg

♛ RUDOLPH I (d 1291) m Anne of Hohenberg

♛ ALBERT I (d 1308)

Rudolph III (d 1307) King of Bohemia — ♛ FREDERICK I 'the Fair' (d 1330) — Leopold I (d 1326)

Rudolph 'the Fair' (d 1365) King of Bohemia — Frederick II (d 1362) — Albert III (d 1395) Archduke of Austria m Beatrice of Nuremberg — Leopold III (d 1386 acquired Styria and Ty

Albert IV (d 1414) — William (d 1406)

♛ ALBERT II (d 1439) — Margaret (d 1486) m Frederick II of Saxony

Anna (d 1462) m William III, Duke of Savoy — Elisabeth (d 1503) m Casimir III, King of Poland — Ladislaus Postumus (d 1457) — ⚜⬡ MAXIMILIAN I (1459–

♙ PHILIP I 'the Fair' (1478–

Eleanor (d 1558) — ⚜⬡ CHARLES V (d 1556) m Isabella of Portugal ♙ (Charles I)

♙ PHILIP II (1527–98) m Anne, daughter of Maximilian II — Marie (d 1603) m Maximilian II — Margaret m Duke of Parma — John of Austria

Don Carlos (d 1568) — Isabella (d 1633) — Catherine (d 1630) m Charles Emmanuel of Savoy — PHILIP III (1578–1621) m Margaret of Styria — ⚜⬡ RUDOLPH (1552–1612

Anna Maria m Louis XIII of France — ♙ PHILIP IV (1605–65) Isabella of France (1) m   m (2) Maria Anne — FERDINAND III (1608– m Marie (1646)

Maria Theresa (1638–83) m Louis XIV of France — ♙ CHARLES II (1661–1700) — Margarita Theresa (d 1673) (i) m LEOPOLD I (1640–170

Louis, Dauphin (1661–1711) — Maria Antonia (1669–92) m Maximilian Emmanuel of Ba

♙ PHILIP V of Bourbon (1683–1746) — Joseph Ferdinand (1692–9

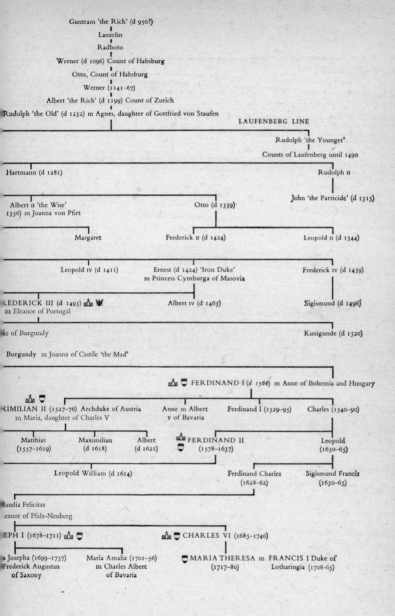

Guntram 'the Rich' (d 950?)

Lanzelin

Radboto

Werner (d 1096) Count of Habsburg

Otto, Count of Habsburg

Werner (1141–67)

Albert 'the Rich' (d 1199) Count of Zurich

Rudolph 'the Old' (d 1232) m Agnes, daughter of Gottfried von Staufen

LAUFENBERG LINE

Rudolph 'the Younger'

Counts of Laufenberg until 1490

Hartmann (d 1281)

Rudolph II

Albert II 'the Wise' 1356) m Joanna von Pfirt

Otto (d 1339)

John 'the Parricide' (d 1315)

Margaret

Frederick II (d 1424)

Leopold II (d 1344)

Leopold IV (d 1411)

Ernest (d 1424) 'Iron Duke' m Princess Cymburga of Masovia

Frederick IV (d 1439)

REDERICK III (d 1493) m Eleanor of Portugal

Albert IV (d 1463)

Sigismund (d 1496)

ic of Burgundy

Kunigunde (d 1520)

Burgundy m Joanna of Castile 'the Mad'

FERDINAND I (d 1566) m Anne of Bohemia and Hungary

KIMILIAN II (1527–76) Archduke of Austria m Maria, daughter of Charles V

Anne m Albert V of Bavaria

Ferdinand I (1529–95)

Charles (1540–90)

Matthias (1557–1619)

Maximilian (d 1618)

Albert (d 1621)

FERDINAND II (1578–1637)

Leopold (1630–65)

Leopold William (d 1614)

Ferdinand Charles (1628–62)

Sigismund Francis (1630–65)

laudia Felicitas

eanor of Pfalz-Neuberg

EPH I (1678–1711)

CHARLES VI (1685–1740)

a Josepha (1699–1757) Frederick Augustus of Saxony

Maria Amalia (1701–56) m Charles Albert of Bavaria

MARIA THERESA m FRANCIS I Duke of (1717–80) Lotharingia (1708–65)

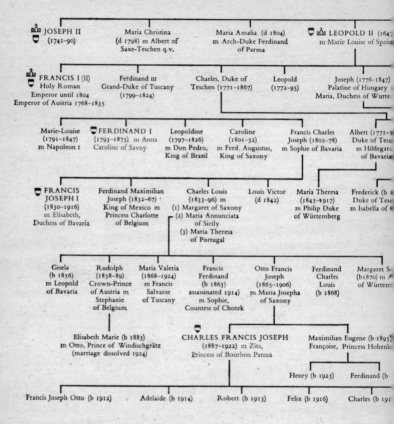

JOSEPH II (1741–90) — Maria Christina (d 1798) m Albert of Saxe-Teschen q.v. — Maria Amalia (d 1804) m Arch-Duke Ferdinand of Parma — LEOPOLD II (164... m Marie Louise of Spain

FRANCIS I (II) Holy Roman Emperor until 1804 Emperor of Austria 1768–1835 — Ferdinand III Grand-Duke of Tuscany (1799–1824) — Charles, Duke of Teschen (1771–1867) — Leopold (1772–95) — Joseph (1776–1847) Palatine of Hungary Maria, Duchess of Wurte...

Marie-Louise (1791–1847) m Napoleon I — FERDINAND I (1793–1875) m Anna Caroline of Savoy — Leopoldine (1797–1826) m Don Pedro, King of Brazil — Caroline (1801–32) m Fred. Augustus, King of Saxony — Francis Charles Joseph (1802–78) m Sophie of Bavaria — Albert (1771–... Duke of Tes... m Hildegard of Bavaria

FRANCIS JOSEPH I (1830–1916) m Elisabeth, Duchess of Bavaria — Ferdinand Maximilian Joseph (1832–67) King of Mexico m Princess Charlotte of Belgium — Charles Louis (1833–96) m (1) Margaret of Saxony (2) Maria Annunciata of Sicily (3) Maria Theresa of Portugal — Louis Victor (d 1842) — Maria Theresa (1845–1917) m Philip Duke of Würtemberg — Frederick (b ... Duke of Tes... m Isabella of ...

Gisela (b 1856) m Leopold of Bavaria — Rudolph (1858–89) Crown-Prince of Austria m Stephanie of Belgium — Maria Valeria (1868–1924) m Francis Salvator of Tuscany — Francis Ferdinand (b 1863) assassinated 1914 m Sophie, Countess of Chotek — Otto Francis Joseph (1865–1906) m Maria Josepha of Saxony — Ferdinand Charles Louis (b 1868) — Margaret S... (b1870) m ... of Würtem...

Elisabeth Marie (b 1883) m Otto, Prince of Windischgrätz (marriage dissolved 1924) — CHARLES FRANCIS JOSEPH (1887–1922) m Zita, Princess of Bourbon Parma — Maximilian Eugene (b 1895) Françoise, Princess Hohenle...

Henry (b 1925) — Ferdinand (b ...

Francis Joseph Otto (b 1912) — Adelaide (b 1914) — Robert (b 1915) — Felix (b 1916) — Charles (b 191...)

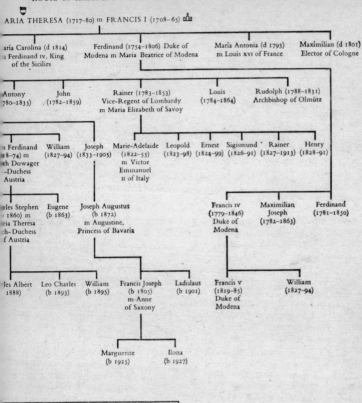

ARIA THERESA (1717–80) m FRANCIS I (1708–65)

aria Carolina (d 1814) m Ferdinand iv, King of the Sicilies — Ferdinand (1754–1806) Duke of Modena m Maria Beatrice of Modena — Maria Antonia (d 1793) m Louis xvi of France — Maximilian (d 1801) Elector of Cologne

Antony (...780–1835) — John (1782–1859) — Rainer (1783–1853) Vice-Regent of Lombardy m Maria Elizabeth of Savoy — Louis (1784–1864) — Rudolph (1788–1831) Archbishop of Olmütz

...s Ferdinand (...8–74) m ...th Dowager -Duchess ...Austria — William (1827–94) — Joseph (1833–1905) — Marie-Adelaide (1822–55) m Victor Emmanuel ii of Italy — Leopold (1823–98) — Ernest (1824–99) — Sigismund (1826–91) — Rainer (1827–1913) — Henry (1828–91)

...les Stephen ...1860) m ...ria Theresa ...h-Duchess ...f Austria — Eugene (b 1863) — Joseph Augustus (b 1872) m Augustine, Princess of Bavaria — Francis iv (1779–1846) Duke of Modena — Maximilian Joseph (1782–1863) — Ferdinand (1781–1850)

...les Albert ...1888) — Leo Charles (b 1893) — William (b 1895) — Francis Joseph (b 1805) m Anne of Saxony — Ladislaus (b 1901) — Francis v (1819–85) Duke of Modena — William (1827–94)

Marguerite (b 1925) — Ilona (b 1927)

...olph Syringus (b 1919) — Charlotte (b 1921) — Elisabeth (b 1922)

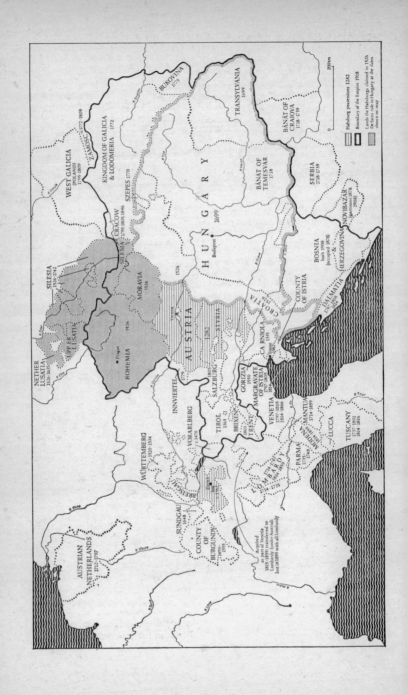

NETHER LUSATIA
1526-1635

UPP LUSATIA
1526-1635

WEST GALICIA
(POLAND)
1795-1809

ZAMOSC
1772-1809

KINGDOM OF GALICIA
& LODOMERIA
1772

BUKOVINA
1775

SZEPES
1770

CRACOW
1795 1809 1846

SILESIA
1526-1742

SILESIA
1526

MORAVIA
1526

BOHEMIA
1526

Prague

AUSTRIAN
NETHERLANDS
1713-1797

R. Rhine

R. Meuse

COUNTY OF
BURGUNDY
1493-1555

SUNDGAU
1648

WÜRTEMBERG
1520-1534

BRISGAU
c.1470

VORARLBERG

INNVIERTEL
1779

TIROL
1363

BRIXEN
1803

TRENT
1801

SALZBURG
1805

Venice

R. Po

R. Tiber

LUCCA

TUSCANY
1737-1801
1814-1816

MODENA
1814-1859

PARMA
1735-
1748

MANTUA
1714-1859

LOMBARDY
1714 1735
1814 1859

VENETIA
1797-1805
1814-1866

Acquired
as part of Venetia
1815-1859; transferred as
Lombardy to Austria,
lost in 1859 with all Lombardy

GORIZIA
1500

MARGRAVATE
OF ISTRIA
1797-1805

Trieste
1382

CARNIOLA
1335

CARINTHIA
1335

COUNTY
OF ISTRIA

DALMATIA
1815

CROATIA

AUSTRIA
1282

STYRIA
1282

R. Drave

HUNGARY
1699

Budapest

R. Danube

R. Theiss

R. Save

R. Maros

BOSNIA
both 1908
(occupied 1878)

HERZEGOVINA
(occupied 1878)

NOVI BAZAR
(garrisons 1878-
1908)

SERBIA
1718-1739

BANAT OF
TEMESVAR
1718

BANAT OF
CRAIOVA
1718-1739

TRANSYLVANIA
1699

200m

○────────●

0

Habsburg possessions 1282
Boundary of the Empire 1526
Lands the Habsburgs claimed in 1526
De facto rule in Hungary at the dates
shown on map

Index

183

Introducing the Transworld Student Library – a series designed to meet the modern educational needs of the independent learner.

THEORETICAL STATISTICS – BASIC IDEAS

Stanley N. Collings
Reader in Statistics, The Open University

Theoretical Statistics does not pretend that statistics is a non-mathematical subject. Starting from a few A-level concepts, and confining itself to discrete situations, it provides a clear introduction to how these concepts are used in formulating the basic ideas upon which probability and sampling notions are built.

0 552 40002 5   100 pages   70p

BOOLEAN ALGEBRA

H. Graham Flegg
Reader in Mathematics, The Open University

Boolean Algebra provides a general introduction from first principles to the algebra of two-state devices through a discussion of sets, propositions and simple switching circuits. The algebra presented here now forms part of most 'modern' mathematics syllabuses and is of considerable importance in a number of fields of application.

0 552 40001 7   160 pages   80p

POINTS AND ARROWS: THE THEORY OF GRAPHS

Arnold Kaufmann
Professor at L'Institut polytechnique de Grenoble
Translated by H. Graham Flegg

Points and Arrows provides a sound elementary introduction to the theory of graphs, a branch of modern mathematics of increasing importance in various sciences, sociology, economics and business studies. Applications to various optimal path problems are discussed, and a fascinating glimpse is provided into recent theories of pattern recognition systems.

0 552 40003 3   160 pages   80p

FIELD PROJECTS IN SOCIOLOGY

Jacqueline P. Wiseman and Marcia S. Aron

Jacqueline P. Wiseman is Assistant Professor of Sociology at San Francisco State College. Marcia S. Aron teaches sociology at the City College of San Francisco.
This book is a practical guide to the study of human group life. It takes the reader out of the library into the field, and explains the methods used by sociologists and other social scientists to explore various aspects of human behaviour and social life. Very little knowledge of sociology is assumed.

0 552 40007 6   336 pages   95p

FORTHCOMING TITLES (December publication)
Meteorology, by H. J. Tanck   144 pages   0 552 40005 X   80p
The Unknown Ego, by Tobias Brocher   112 pages   0 552 40006 8   75p
Calculus Via Numerical Analysis, by A. Graham and G. Read   96 pages   0 552 40008 4   70p
Reliability: A Mathematical Approach, by Arnold Kaufmann   96 pages   0 552 40009 2   70p

A SELECTION OF FINE READING AVAILABLE IN CORGI BOOKS

War

☐ 552 09042 5 **THE LUFTWAFFE DIARIES (illustrated)** *Cajus Becker* 60p
☐ 552 09055 7 **SIDESHOW** *Gerard Bell* 30p
☐ 552 09041 7 **ALL STATIONS TO MALTA** *Gilbert Hackforth-Jones* 30p
☐ 552 08874 9 **SS GENERAL** *Sven Hassel* 35p
☐ 552 08779 3 **ASSIGNMENT: GESTAPO** *Sven Hassel* 35p
☐ 552 08855 2 **THE WILLING FLESH** *Willi Heinrich* 35p
☐ 552 08993 1 **ONCE THERE WAS A WAR** *John Steinbeck* 25p
☐ 552 08986 9 **DUEL OF EAGLES (illustrated)** *Peter Townsend* 50p
☐ 552 08936 2 **JOHNNY GOT HIS GUN** *Dalton Trumbo* 30p
☐ 552 09004 2 **THE LONG WATCH** *Alan White* 25p
☐ 552 09014 X **THE LONG NIGHT'S WALK** *Alan White* 30p

Romance

☐ 552 09008 5 **SHADOWS ON THE WATER** *Elizabeth Cadell* 25p
☐ 552 09043 3 **CANARY YELLOW** *Elizabeth Cadell* 30p
☐ 552 09060 3 **SISTER CARLIN'S SUCCESSOR** *Hilary Neal* 25p
☐ 552 09029 8 **A SUNSET TOUCH** *Alex Stuart* 25p

Science Fiction

☐ 552 08925 7 **THE BEST FROM NEW WRITINGS IN S.F.**
ed. *John Carnell* 25p
☐ 552 09061 1 **LION OF COMARRE** *Arthur C. Clarke* 30p
☐ 552 08942 7 **A WILDERNESS OF STARS** ed. *William Nolan* 30p
☐ 552 08860 9 **VENUS PLUS X** *Theodore Sturgeon* 25p

General

☐ 552 09009 3 **A RAP ON RACE** *James Baldwin and Margaret Mead* 40p
☐ 552 08944 3 **BILLY CASPER'S 'MY MILLION-DOLLAR SHOTS'** 50p
☐ 552 08926 5 **S IS FOR SEX** *Robert Chartham* 50p
☐ 552 98958 4 **THE ISLAND RACE Vol. 1** *Winston S. Churchill* 125p
☐ 552 98959 2 **THE ISLAND RACE Vol. 2** *Winston S. Churchill* 125p
☐ 552 09011 5 **GEHLEN: SPY OF THE CENTURY (illustrated)**
E. H. Cookridge 50p
☐ 552 08800 5 **CHARIOTS OF THE GODS? (illustrated)** *Erich von Daniken* 35p
☐ 552 07400 4 **MY LIFE AND LOVES** *Frank Harris* 65p
☐ 552 98748 4 **MAKING LOVE (Photographs)** *Walter Hartford* 85p
☐ 552 08992 3 **MASTERING WITCHCRAFT** *Paul Huson* 35p
☐ 552 98862 6 **INVESTING IN GEORGIAN GLASS (illustrated)**
Ward Lloyd 125p
☐ 552 09062 X **THE SENSUOUS MAN** *"M"* 35p
☐ 552 08069 1 **THE OTHER VICTORIANS** *Steven Marcus* 50p
☐ 552 09030 1 **BORN TO HEAL (illustrated)** *Paul Miller* 35p
☐ 552 08010 1 **THE NAKED APE** *Desmond Morris* 30p
☐ 552 09044 1 **SEX ENERGY** *Robert S. de Ropp* 35p
☐ 552 09016 6 **GOLF TACTICS** *Arnold Palmer* 45p
☐ 552 08880 3 **THE THIRTEENTH CANDLE** *T. Lobsang Rampa* 35p
☐ 552 08974 5 **BRUCE TEGNER METHOD OF SELF DEFENCE** 40p
☐ 552 09059 X **BEHIND THE MASK OF TUTANKHAMEN** *Barry Wynne* 35p

Western

☐ 552 08194 9   No. 44 THE WILDCATS   *J. T. Edson* 25p

☐ 552 08971 0   TO ARMS! TO ARMS IN DIXIE No. 68   *J. T. Edson* 25p

☐ 552 08972 9   THE SOUTH WILL RISE AGAIN No. 69   *J. T. Edson* 25p

☐ 552 08995 8   CATLOW   *Louis L'Amour* 25p

☐ 552 09027 1   SACKETT   *Louis L'Amour* 25p

☐ 552 09006 9   CALLAGHEN   *Louis L'Amour* 30p

☐ 552 09058 1   RIDE THE DARK TRAIL   *Louis L'Amour* 25p

☐ 552 09048 4   RIO GRANDE   *Louis Masterson* 25p

☐ 552 08990 7   RETURN TO ACTION No. 16   *Louis Masterson* 25p

☐ 552 09007 7   MONTE WALSH   *Jack Schaefer* 40p

☐ 552 09064 6   SUDDEN RIDES AGAIN   *Oliver Strange* 25p

Crime

☐ 552 09024 7   THE GALLOWS ARE WAITING   *John Creasey* 25p

☐ 552 09025 5   'WARE DANGER   *John Creasey* 25p

☐ 552 08640 1   RED FILE FOR CALLAN   *James Mitchell* 30p

☐ 552 08937 0   THE KNIVES OF JUSTICE   *Mildred Savage* 50p

☐ 552 09005 0   SONNTAG   *Michael Sinclair* 30p

☐ 552 08883 8   THE BIG KILL   *Mickey Spillane* 25p

☐ 552 09056 5   SHAFT   *Ernest Tidyman* 30p

☐ 552 09072 7   SHAFT'S BIG SCORE   *Ernest Tidyman* 30p

All these books are available at your bookshop or newsagent: or can be ordered direct from the publisher. Just tick the titles you want and fill in the form below.

CORGI BOOKS, Cash Sales Department, P.O. Box 11, Falmouth, Cornwall.
Please send cheque or postal order. No currency, and allow 6p per book to cover the cost of postage and packing in the U.K., and overseas.

NAME ....

ADDRESS ....

(OCT 72) ....